GOING SOLO

A simple guide to soaring

GOING SOLO

A simple guide to soaring

Derek Piggott

A & C Black · London

A & C Black (Publishers) Ltd
35 Bedford Row, London WC1R 4JH

First published 1978
Reprinted 1984, 1987

Piggott, Derek
  Going solo.
  1. Gliding and soaring
  I. Title
629.132′523   TL765
ISBN 0-7136-1899-x

Filmset and printed in Great Britain by
BAS Printers Limited, Over Wallop, Hampshire

Contents

Illustrations

Introduction

The excitement and fascination of soaring flight must be experienced to be appreciated. On a summer's day huge warm buoyant bubbles of air are continually leaving the ground to form thermals, rising currents of air which a glider pilot can use to gain height. These invisible air currents often rise hundreds of feet a minute, carrying the glider with them up to the little white cumulus clouds at four or five thousand feet. By circling inside the thermal, adjusting the position of the glider until it is in the strongest part of the up-current, the glider pilot gains his height before setting off in search of the next area of lift.

Thermals occur almost everywhere on a fine sunny day, but the airflow over hills and mountain ranges also provides a source of rising air. In this case, unlike thermal activity, the strength and direction of the wind is the most important factor. Hill lift was the first form of lift used by gliders and many of the older gliding sites are on hills. Wave lift occurs in some circumstances when the airflow over hills or mountains takes up a wave motion, producing strong up-currents capable of taking gliders up to twenty or thirty thousand feet. Since hill and wave soaring do not depend on the sun's heat they are possible in the winter, which makes it an all the year round sport.

The modern glider pilot tries to master all ways of soaring. Each has its particular fascination, but the majority of flights are made in thermals and on a good day a skilled pilot can cover two or three hundred miles.

This kind of flying may seem remote to you if you are only just starting to learn. It is difficult to comprehend that if you fly regularly you will be solo in a few weeks or months. Once you are solo it is only a matter of practice before you will be making flights of hours instead of minutes.

1

FACTS AND FORMALITIES

Training, licences and formalities, facts about gliders

Every glider pilot will tell you that soaring is the greatest sport. The flying, of course, is wonderful but we cannot all be in the air together. There must be wingtip holders, tug pilots, signallers, tow car or winch drivers and others willing and able to help push your glider out to the launch point or back for another flight. Alternatively, someone must be paid to do the work, making your gliding much more expensive. Rich or poor, you alone can decide whether this is worth your while. If you want to be able to book your flying and have the aircraft waiting for you to step into, then you should go to your nearest power flying club.

If you decide that you want to learn to glide, this little book will give you most of the information you will need as you start your training.

Training

There are various ways in which you can learn to glide. It will not take very long if you are already a power pilot. But in any case it is a good plan to visit your nearest gliding clubs, talk to the members and have at least one flight *before* you commit yourself to joining as a full flying member. If you are discouraged by finding that you must wait your turn to fly and that even as a prospective member you will not receive any special priority, then perhaps club gliding is not the sport for you. Give up the idea now, rather than begin overenthusiastically only to lose interest after a few flights.

Training can either be on a casual day-to-day basis as a member of a gliding club, or on a residential course of a week or longer. Two or three weeks of training may get you solo but it is only by flying regularly that you will become really proficient. Eventually, that means becoming an active member of a club.

Licences and formalities

In Great Britain there are very few restrictions placed on the glider pilot. No glider pilot's licence is required but there are internationally recognised certificates and badges to mark the pilot's progress. Most other countries have glider pilot's licences involving a medical, and flying and ground examinations similar to those for a Private Power Pilot Licence. In addition each pilot keeps a personal log book and the entries and comments by instructors give a good indication of the pupil's competence. However, even an experienced pilot would expect to make at least one dual check flight at a new site or club before flying solo there.

Provided that you are reasonably healthy and do not suffer from epilepsy, blackouts or fainting fits and have average eyesight (if necessary with glasses) you are almost certainly fit to glide. At some clubs you may be asked to get your doctor to sign a statement to this effect.

As you gain experience you will have to learn about the special rules of the air regarding airways etc., but this need not worry you until you are solo and are beginning to think about flying across country.

The first step is to learn to fly the glider.

Facts about gliders

It is not within the scope of this book to explain in detail exactly how and why an aeroplane or glider flies. In fact it is not really essential for you to understand more than the fundamentals, since learning to glide is mainly a practical affair.

Most of the necessary information you will pick up during your training. If you know how the controls work and a little about how an aeroplane flies, you know more than enough for your first few flights.

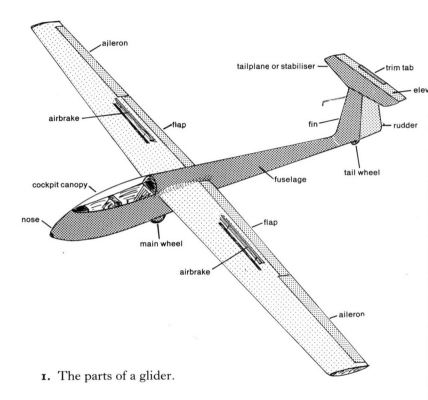

1. The parts of a glider.

Figure 1 shows the main parts of a glider. The long span and short chord of the wings give the glider the high lift and very low drag necessary for a flat glide and low rate of descent. Very careful attention is paid to streamlining in order to keep the drag to a minimum to obtain a good gliding performance. Gliders are designed to very stringent airworthiness requirements and are structurally very strong. They are usually built to withstand loads over five times greater than normal flying loads at speeds of over 120 mph, and they can perform simple aerobatics such as loops, chandelles and spins. Landing shocks are taken by the mainwheel and tailwheel or skid under the tail. On high performance machines the main wheel is invariably retracted in flight to reduce the drag. Training aircraft and many other medium performance gliders have a fixed main wheel and an additional nose skid to absorb the shocks of a bad nose-down landing on rough ground.

The wings and tailplane of gliders can be quickly removed to allow the glider to be retrieved by road in a long trailer.

2

THE GLIDER

The controls, how an aeroplane flies, flying speed, turning, launching, performance

The controls

The cockpit and main controls of a glider are identical to those of any other aircraft and consist of the stick (or control column) and the rudder pedals. (Fig. 2.) The stick is always held in the *right* hand and both feet are rested against the rudder pedals. Forward and backward movements of the stick operate the *elevator* and result in nose down and nose up *pitching* movements. Movements to the left or right operate the *ailerons* out on the wing tips and these control surfaces move in opposite directions. A movement to the left on the stick moves the aileron on the left wingtip up, and the one on the right wingtip down. The left wingtip loses a little lift and the right wingtip gains a little additional lift, resulting in a *rolling* or *banking* to the left. (Fig. 3.) The movements of the stick soon become instinctive. You lean or press the stick in the direction you want the glider to go, so you press the stick forward to put the nose down. Move the stick to the left to bank over to the left.

The rudder movements are not instinctive. Left foot forward moves the rudder surface to the left and swings or *yaws* the nose to the left. Right foot or right rudder swings the nose to the right. If the rudder is applied and held on while the wings are kept level, the nose swings a little to the side and then stops swinging. The glider skids sideways through the air as if skating on ice and scarcely changes direction. When the rudder is centralised again the nose swings back and the aircraft returns to accurate straight flight. Sideways move-

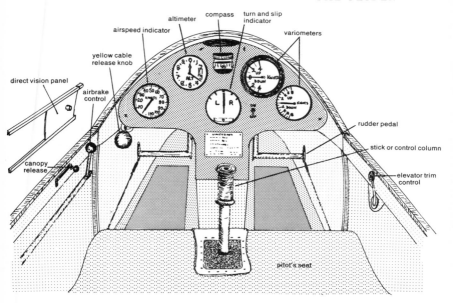

2. A typical cockpit layout for a two-seater training glider.

ments like this result in the fuselage creating much more drag and there is very little tendency to turn. For efficient flight the rudder is used to *prevent* any sideways slipping or skidding, particularly as the glider is changing its angle of bank.

The glider is always banked over to make it turn and once it is turning very little rudder is required. Flat unbanked turns are practically impossible.

In smooth air the glider can be made to fly 'hands and feet off' and it will continue flying steadily by itself. In more turbulent conditions the glider is disturbed from time to time and the pilot has to make corrections to bring the wings level and occasionally to reposition the nose in the correct attitude. But it is stable and tends to correct itself if allowed to do so. During early flights students invariably become too tense, make jerky movements and over-control. The glider will often fly far better if the pilot relaxes on the controls and allows the natural stability of the glider to work.

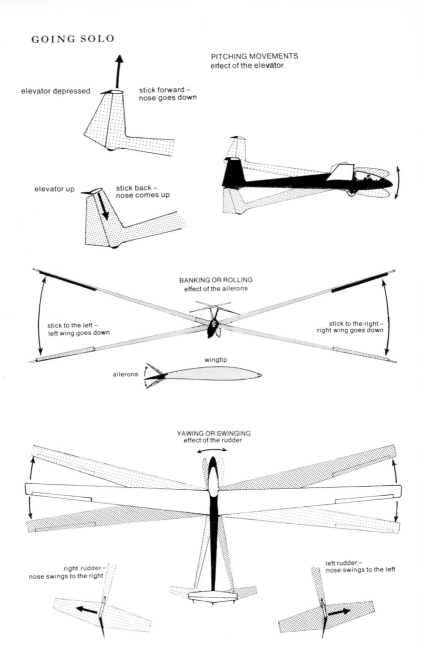

3. The controls and their effects. The elevator controls pitching movements, the ailerons rolling or banking, and the rudder yawing.

How an aeroplane flies

With a powered aircraft, the thrust from the engine or propeller drives the aircraft through the air to overcome the resistance we call drag. If there is sufficient flying speed the wing generates enough lift to support the weight. The tail keeps the wing steady and the fuselage pointing accurately in the line of flight so that there is no unnecessary drag.

Flying speed

The lift from the wings depends on the speed of the airflow over them and on the angle of attack (the angle at which the wing meets the airflow). If the speed is high enough, lift is created at a small angle of attack and the aircraft flies rather nose down. At low speeds the wing is pulled to a larger angle of attack and the aircraft is rather nose high. (Fig. 4.) In reality the speed and angle of attack are controlled by the elevator.

Beyond a certain angle the wing becomes very inefficient

4. Flying at high and low speeds. Notice the nose high attitude and the larger angle of attack of the wing at low speed.

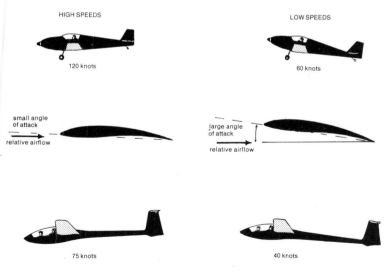

HIGH SPEEDS

LOW SPEEDS

120 knots

60 knots

small angle
of attack

large angle
of attack

relative airflow

relative airflow

75 knots

40 knots

and the lift decreases so that there is a definite limit as to how slowly each type of aircraft can fly. For this reason a glider has to maintain a minimum speed of about 40 knots or 45 mph.

Flying is, in some respects, rather like cycling. In level flight or on level ground, power is required to overcome the drag and to maintain speed. In gliding flight the speed is maintained by descending the glide slope, much like freewheeling down a hill. As the weight of the glider must be supported by lift a certain minimum speed is essential for steady flight. In steady flight the airspeed depends on the attitude, which is controlled by the elevator (the stick movements forwards or backwards).

Turning

The aircraft is turned by banking the wings so that the lift

5. Turning. The turning force is provided by banking over and easing back on the stick. This pulls the wings to a slightly larger angle of attack to provide more lift.

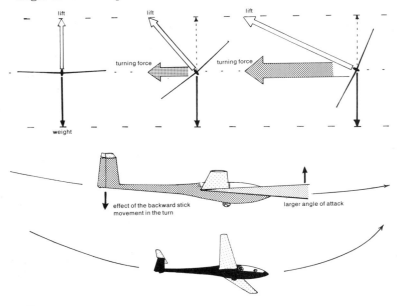

force acts at an angle, thus pulling the aircraft round in the turn. In a turn the wing still has to support the weight, but in addition it provides the turning force so that more lift is required for a turn. This is obtained by making a small backward movement of the stick to pull the wing to a larger angle relative to the airflow. (Fig. 5.)

Launching

Briefly, gliders are usually launched by towing them up to height with a light aircraft. They can also be launched by catapult (bungee), or with a winch, or towing by motor car. Once the tow has been released, the gliders drift down, losing height gradually, unless they are flown into an area of rising air. From a 2000 foot launch height a training glider will take about 10 to 15 minutes to glide down for a landing. In soaring conditions however the flight can be extended for as long as the weather remains favourable.

Performance

Most training gliders have a normal flying speed of about 45 knots (50 mph) and a maximum permissible speed in a dive of about 120 knots. In many countries knots or nautical miles per hour are used in preference to miles an hour or kilometres per hour. 1 knot is almost exactly equal to 100 feet per minute and by using these units it is possible to make quick estimates of the gliding performance. For example, if the rate of descent is 3 knots or 300 feet per minute and the airspeed is 60 knots, the gliding angle is $60 \div 3 = 20:1$. This means that the glider will fly a distance of 20 times its height or, in no wind, just under 4 miles per thousand feet of height lost.

The normal rate of descent of most gliders is 150 to 200 feet per minute ($1\frac{1}{2}$ to 2 knots) at a speed of about 45 knots. At higher speeds, of course, the glider is gliding much more steeply and the rate of sink is far greater.

3

BEFORE YOUR FIRST FLIGHT

When to go gliding, sensations, cockpit checks, your seating position

When to go gliding

If you can choose on which days you are going to go gliding, always listen to the radio or look at the weather forecast and try to avoid obviously bad weather. For your first few flights, you need good conditions to make quick progress. Do not go gliding if the forecast is for gales, rain or hill fog. Strong winds usually mean bumpy conditions and these are best avoided until you have done several flights and are used to handling the controls. Rain makes gliding unpleasant since everyone gets wet. You cannot see clearly and the performance of all gliders is spoiled by the effect of water on the wing, so gliders are not normally flown in rain. Any dry day with a light wind and without low cloud will be ideal for learning. Unfortunately, at a soaring club a really good day will attract all the more experienced pilots—which leaves fewer launches for instructional flying.

If you arrive and the weather is too bad to fly, you can learn useful things by helping in the hangar or by listening to the other pilots chatting over a cup of tea. There may be talks and discussions by the instructors and you will probably be welcome to join in and listen even if, as on weekdays, they are primarily for course members. Go to as many talks as you can as this will save you time and money.

Remember that drinking and flying do not mix and if you do have any alcoholic drinks, then you certainly should not fly solo. Whereas you may be able to drive fairly safely after a few drinks, research shows that ability to fly is seriously affected

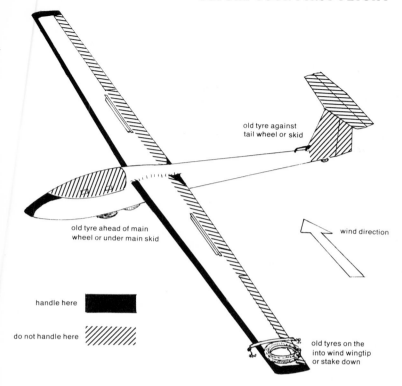

old tyre against
tail wheel or skid

old tyre ahead of main
wheel or under main skid

wind direction

handle here

do not handle here

old tyres on the
into wind wingtip
or stake down

6. Ground handling. It is easy to damage an aircraft by bad ground handling. Gliders are parked at right angles to the wind and are never left unattended unless they are properly parked.

by *any* alcohol and that the effects last 10–12 hours or more. So even if the weather looks hopeless at lunch time, it is best to stick to soft drinks in case of an improvement later on.

When you arrive at the gliding site, before you do *anything else* put your name on the flying list. If you are first to arrive, start a flying list yourself, even if the weather looks doubtful. The flying list is the order of flying, so no name—no fly! Then offer to help with the gliders. Figure 6 shows which parts must not be handled, but if you are not sure ask the pilot or the instructor in charge.

The training at most gliding clubs is on two-seater gliders, but it can also be done on a motor glider, as at the Lasham Gliding Centre. Changing from one type of glider to another or from gliders to motor gliders from flight to flight will be like trying to learn to drive using a car for some lessons and a truck for others. It makes it all rather difficult and confusing.

The motor glider is vastly superior for learning how to land and can extend its flights if required. Instead of a turn of 2 or 3 launches on the glider, you can get 8 landings in a 30-minute session in the motor glider and it is practice you need. Naturally you will be keen to progress to real gliders, but be patient because you will learn more quickly in the motor glider and an extra day or so on it can save you many days of training on the glider.

All two-seater training machines have full dual control so that the instructor can take over in an instant if you need help at any stage. In smooth air the glider will fly 'hands off' without assistance. It is stable and is not about to fall out of the sky, although it may feel like it.

Sensations

On your first few flights you will experience some vivid and occasionally worrying sensations. This is quite normal and you will find that after a few flights the sensations become less and less noticeable. An aeroplane is often tipped slightly by bumps in the air, so that even if you hold the controls still it does not continue in steady flight. This means that the pilot has to make some corrections on the controls to keep the glider in level flight. Eventually you will learn to recognise these bumps and to correct for them, when they happen, smoothly and automatically.

While you are still getting used to the controls, these bumps are rather disconcerting and it will be difficult for you to tell, for example, whether the glider is banking over rather quickly because of a bump lifting one wing or whether it is because of a movement you have made on the controls. Sometimes a bump will tip you one way, sometimes the other. A small movement on the stick to apply some bank for a turn may have no effect at all for a few seconds if a bump is opposing the control movement, whereas on another occasion a small movement may result in a rapid banking movement into quite a steep turn. This can be rather alarming and is bound to be confusing until the control movements have become more or less instinctive.

These sensations and how and why they occur are explained in the author's *Beginning Gliding* (A. & C. Black). Briefly, any nose-down pitching movement of the glider or any turbulence causing the glider suddenly to sink a few feet produces an unpleasant feeling, similar to that felt when driving over a hump-backed bridge or in an elevator or lift. After a few flights this feeling decreases because when we lower the nose and as we look ahead and see the movement against the horizon, our brain suppresses the sensation which we have learned to expect.

You will also notice that on some occasions as you bank the glider over into a turn you get a vivid feeling that the banking movement is getting out of control. This impression of overbanking and falling towards the lower wing can be very unnerving. This will not happen after a few more flights as it is caused by failing to use the rudder correctly at the start of the turn. Also with a little more practice, you can see that the angle of bank is not getting too steep. Once again your eyesight helps your brain to suppress the sensation and it ceases to be a problem.

We all have an inborn fear of falling, and our senses of balance are primarily to protect us from toppling over and hurting ourselves. Normally the sensations are suppressed by our eyesight, which confirms that all is well. After a few flights have made you familiar with the three-dimensional movements of an aircraft, the eyesight once again becomes the master of the situation so that as long as you can see what is happening the sensations are scarcely noticeable. Contrary to your expectations you will not experience the same sensation of height as when you look down from a cliff or high building.

Cockpit checks

A routine check ensures that nothing vital can be missed and that the pilot can take off without a nagging fear that perhaps he has forgotten something. In Great Britain this take off check is standardised for gliders and is remembered by the mnemonic CB SIFT CB. Each letter stands for a particular item. Other countries have similar checks and you should ask your instructor for details. These checks *must* be learned by heart.

C–Controls–check for full and free movement of the stick and rudder and that these controls are all working correctly.

B–Ballast–check that the cockpit loads (pilot weight plus the weight of the parachute) are within the limits on the cockpit placard. Additional ballast is *vital* if the pilot's weight is less than the prescribed minimum (note: gliders of the same type do not necessarily have the same minimum or maximum cockpit loads).

S–Straps–check that your safety harness (and that of any passengers) is tight.

I–Instruments–check that there are no obvious errors or broken glasses in the critical instruments and reset the altimeter if necessary.

F–Flaps–Set the flaps, if fitted, for take off. (Flaps are not always fitted to training aircraft and this is sometimes omitted).

T–Trimmer–The trim lever should be checked for full and free movement and set to the appropriate position for take off—on most gliders it is central for wire launches and slightly forward for aerotow.

C–Canopy–check the canopy lock and push up in the centre of the canopy to check that the whole canopy is secure.

B–Brakes–check by pulling the airbrake lever fully open and seeing that the airbrakes are open on both wings. *Then close and lock them.*

Once this check has been completed the launching rope or cable can be attached and the glider is ready to be launched.

In a motor glider the instructor operates the engine and checks any additional items such as fuel, switches, etc.

Seating position

As far as possible you should always sit in the same position each time you fly, so that your view ahead is identical. If you are very small, you will need extra padding behind you and perhaps under you to be able to reach all the controls easily. If you are rather short in the leg it may be worth bringing your own cushions. Firm ones are best and a collection of old cardboard boxes folded flat and covered in brown paper or cloth is ideal. You should be able to obtain full rudder movement either way without having to straighten your knees completely and you should also be able to hold the airbrake lever and cable release knob without stretching.

4

EARLY FLIGHTS

The correct flying attitude, using the controls, trimming, turns, the landing

The correct flying attitude

During the early flights you must try to keep the glider flying in the correct attitude and speed for efficiency by looking ahead and learning to recognise the correct position of the nose in relation to the horizon. By looking ahead you can detect both nose up and down and banking movements. Do not look at the wingtips or you will find the nose position changing unnoticed. If the attitude is correct, the speed is correct, the glider is flying efficiently and the handling will be normal; if the nose is too high, the speed will be too slow, the controls will be sluggish and ineffective and the glider will mush down losing height rather quickly. If the nose is too low, the glider will be diving at a high speed and losing height rapidly.

Notice that whereas any change in attitude (nose position) can be seen and corrected immediately, both the airspeed indicator and the sound of the airflow have a considerable time lag. This is because the glider gains or loses speed gradually, quite a few seconds after any change of attitude. (In the same way, a bicycle freewheeling onto a steeper slope takes time to gain speed.)

If you look ahead and see the nose dropping, it is usually possible to bring it back to the correct position long before there is any change in the airspeed. Notice that the speed is always controlled by the attitude. Even in the motor glider or a normal aircraft the engine power has little effect on the speed. If the nose is high the speed is low even at full power. Conversely, even with the engine switched off, a nose down position results in a high speed. The attitude controls the speed and the power controls the rate of climb or descent.

Using the controls

On your first or second flight you will be shown how each control works. The stick movements are easy to remember. You press, or lean the stick in the direction you want the aircraft to go, press the nose down, pull the nose up, lean the stick to the left and the left wing will go down, etc. However, the rudder movements (your foot pedals) are not instinctive; left foot forward swings or yaws the nose to the left and right foot forward yaws the nose to the right. Moreover, the rudder controls on most gliders have very little proper feel and do not tend to centre themselves. Car drivers often find that they fail to move the glider rudder sufficiently with their right foot,

7. The normal gliding attitude. The exact position will vary with your seating position and with each type of aircraft.

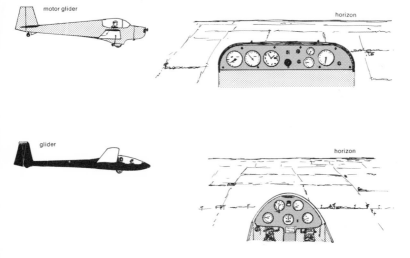

27

probably because in a car the right foot has the more delicate job of controlling the accelerator. A common fault at first is to brace both feet so firmly on the rudders that pressing on one pedal has little or no effect. As you push on one foot, the other foot must be moved back to allow the rudder to move.

There are several points to remember about the effects of the controls. Notice that any forward movement on the stick to lower the nose gives you that nasty hump-backed bridge feeling. Be gentle. The elevator is very powerful and sensitive. The size of a sideways movement of the stick controls the rate of roll and not the angle of bank—e.g. a small move to the left will result in a slow rolling movement to the left, with the angle of bank getting steeper and steeper until the pilot makes a countermove to stop it. A large move to the left will give a rapid rolling movement which again will continue until the pilot makes a countermove to stop it—in other words to bank to a certain angle the pilot initiates the banking by moving the stick, and then stops it with a countermove when it reaches the angle he wants. Turns can only be made by banking the glider.

Trimming

All gliders have some degree of fore and aft stability which means that if they are trimmed to fly 'hands off' at a particular speed, they will always tend to return to that speed after being disturbed. When the glider is correctly trimmed the pilot can relax without the need for constant corrections on the elevator.

The first essential is to adjust the attitude until the glider is flying steadily at the desired speed. Remember to make only small changes in attitude and to wait for the speed to settle down. Then relax your hold of the stick just enough to detect whether the nose is tending to rise or fall, but correct it immediately. Hold the correct attitude and readjust the trim lever a little at a time until there is apparently no forward or backward pressure remaining on the stick. Test the trimming by relaxing once again. If the glider is correctly trimmed it will fly 'hands off' with the speed and attitude remaining constant. It is useful to practise trimming at various speeds until you can do it quickly. Always retrim at any time you notice any constant load on the stick; it is easier to fly a well trimmed glider. Never move the trimmer in flight unless your other hand is holding the stick. Nose heaviness is corrected by moving the trim lever further back; i.e. it works on the same principle as the stick movement.

Remember, do not attempt to retrim the glider exactly unless you have it flying at the correct speed and attitude. It must be in steady flight at the time.

Turns

Because of the low flying speed and large span of a glider, the rudder has to be used in conjunction with the stick movement (sideways) to apply and to take off the bank when entering and coming out of turns. During the turn, very, very little rudder is required, but a small backward move is needed on the stick to prevent the nose dropping and to ensure that the glider maintains the same speed. It is surprisingly difficult to make the rudder movements correctly in harmony with the stick movements and many beginners find it easiest to think aloud about the moves.

To turn correctly (Fig. 8.)

Look around and particularly behind in the direction you are going to turn; *then look ahead* and correct the position of the nose if it is too high or too low; apply the bank with the stick and rudder together (stick to the left with left rudder, i.e. left foot forward), check the bank with a countermove sideways on the stick just beyond the central position to stop the bank increasing, and *then* reduce the rudder to leave a very small amount of rudder in the direction of the turn (left rudder in a left turn). Finally ease back on the stick to prevent the nose dropping as the turn continues.

During a continuous turn use sideways moves on the stick

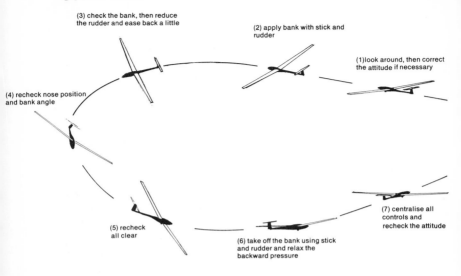

(3) check the bank, then reduce the rudder and ease back a little

(2) apply bank with stick and rudder

(1) look around, then correct the attitude if necessary

(4) recheck nose position and bank angle

(7) centralise all controls and recheck the attitude

(5) recheck all clear

(6) take off the bank using stick and rudder and relax the backward pressure

8. How to turn.

1. Look around and behind for other aircraft, and recheck the attitude.
2. Watching ahead, apply the bank with stick and rudder together.
3. Check the bank with the stick and *then* reduce the rudder.
4. Recheck the nose position and the angle of bank.
5. Recheck it is all clear to continue turning.
6. Take off the bank using the stick and rudder together and relax the backward pressure on the stick.
7. Centralise the stick and rudder as the wings come level and recheck the attitude and speed.

to correct small changes in the angle of bank, and changes in forward or backward pressures to maintain the correct position of the nose in relation to the horizon. Look around several times in each circle. As you come out of the turn, take off the bank by leaning the stick the way you want the aircraft to go, using the rudder at the same time—i.e. stick to the right with right foot forward. As the wings come level relax the backward pressure on the stick so that the attitude remains normal and centralise both stick and rudder together.

Simplifying this: look around and behind, look ahead, stick and rudder together, check the bank with the stick *and then* reduce the rudder, ease back to stop the nose dropping. Check the angle of bank and nose position, check that you have reduced the rudder, look around. Take off the bank with the stick and rudder together, relax the backward pressure and centralise the stick and rudder as the wings come level. You could do far worse than learn these movements off parrot fashion and say them to yourself as you make each turn.

Note that the stick and rudder are moved exactly together as the bank is applied and taken off, and at any time you are bringing the wings level after being tipped by a bump. Small sideways movements of the stick need small rudder movements but larger movements of the stick (to apply or take off the bank quickly) necessitate larger rudder movements. However you never need a large amount of rudder during *any* turn. Turns are really a matter of the bank and backward pressure on the stick and once established in the turn these are the essential movements. In gliders the rudder is used to stop any tendency to swing sideways as bank is applied or taken off.

The rudder movements are the real problem and continue to give every beginner trouble throughout his training.

Notice that you must relax one foot as you push the other. If you brace on one foot and push hard on the other it will feel as though you are moving the pedals, but in fact you are only stretching the cables and the rudder itself will hardly move at all. Everyone becomes very tense at times and most people find that they are not moving the rudder nearly enough.

If you fail to use the rudder or use very little movement as you start to turn, any reduction in movement will leave the glider turning with far too little rudder, i.e. with the wrong rudder on and a slipping movement. Reducing the rudder too soon also causes this slipping movement. This can be detected by a sensation of falling towards the lower wing and a feeling that the glider is tipping over into a steeper and steeper bank. Always check the banking movement with stick first, then immediately afterwards reduce the rudder to leave a little in the direction of the turn.

Some types of glider suffer from a tendency for the rudder to overbalance during inaccurate turns. This gives a beginner the confusing and misleading impression that the instructor is interfering with the rudder control. For example, if too little rudder is applied at the start of the turn, as the glider starts to slip the rudder will be moved over by the airflow so that the pedal pushes against your foot. Similarly if too much rudder

9. Adverse yaw. If the bank is applied without using any rudder, the nose swings the wrong way for a few seconds causing sideslipping motion towards the lower wing. As the angle of bank is checked with the aileron, this sideslipping becomes an almost normal turn.

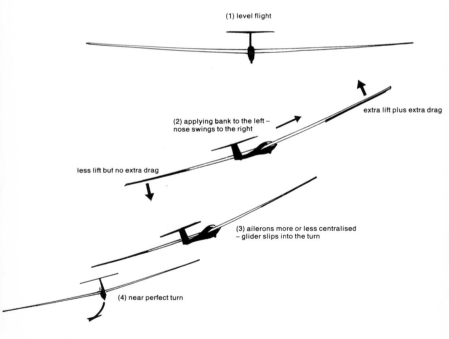

(1) level flight

extra lift plus extra drag

(2) applying bank to the left – nose swings to the right

less lift but no extra drag

(3) ailerons more or less centralised – glider slips into the turn

(4) near perfect turn

is left on during a turn, it will tend to move further, with the same result.

These effects do not occur if the rudder is used correctly. Always push back against any tendency for the rudder to move as this will bring the glider back into accurate flight.

On an early flight you should be shown exactly why the combined stick and rudder movements are necessary. There is a distinct tendency for the glider to swing to the right as the stick is moved to the left to apply bank to the left. This swing is called *adverse yaw*, and is the effect of aileron drag. (Fig. 9.) It occurs whenever the stick is moved sideways to apply or take off bank and is very noticeable in gliders because of their long wing spans and very low flying speeds. Aileron drag is scarcely detectable in a modern powered aeroplane and therefore the rudder is not required for turns in these aircraft. Whereas the amount of rudder movement needed scarcely varies for different angles of bank, the amount of backward movement on the stick needed in a turn *is* dependent on the angle of bank. It is the backward movement which pulls the wing to a slightly larger angle which produces the additional lift required for the turn. Gentle turns require very little extra lift, whereas steep turns need much more. You will notice that if you fail to ease back, the nose drops gradually in a gentle turn, but more quickly in a steeper one. Remember to relax forward again as you bring the wings level to straighten up, or when changing from one turn to another.

Judging the attitude during a turn is a relatively simple matter in a tandem seater aircraft, whereas with side by side seating the position of the nose will appear to change depending on which direction you are turning. Look at your side of the nose as you apply the bank and try to ignore the apparent change of the vertical attitude of the nose. The width of the nose makes it easier to see any banking movements in a side by side trainer than in a tandem seater. In fact, these differences become insignificant after a few flights.

The normal attitude and cruising speed is enough for turns using angles of bank up to about 40°, which is steeper than you will normally use. Very steep turns require an extra 5 knots or so because stalling speed is much higher in a steep turn.

The landing

With motor glider training it is usual to make a start on the landings after two or three trips of handling and practising turns. It is an easy matter to do 7 or 8 landings in a half-hour session, and you soon learn how to land.

With 'all glider' training most instructors begin to teach the landing straight after instruction on how the controls work as it is difficult to get enough practice. At first the instructor takes care of the circuit planning and the use of the airbrakes, leaving the student to concentrate on his turns and then on the landing itself. It is much easier for the student if the use of the airbrakes is not introduced until the landings are reasonably consistent.

It is quite normal to find that as you start to concentrate on the approach and landings, your co-ordination deteriorates for a while. This causes the glider to swing about instead of flying straight.

Later, when you start the circuit planning and the use of the airbrakes you will probably find to your dismay that you cannot get the glider to fly where you want it to go. This is quite normal and is caused by forgetting to use the rudder. Once again, after a few more flights you will overcome this problem, so do not feel discouraged.

Whereas everyone has a problem in learning to use the rudder correctly in conjunction with the stick movements, it is unusual to have much real trouble over learning to land. It is difficult and takes a great deal of practice to form the habit of using feet and hands together automatically, whereas landing is a normal learning problem.

No two landings are identical and the pilot has to learn to watch ahead and see how the aircraft is responding to his control movements. It takes practice, and this is more difficult to come by for a glider pupil who is doing 2 or 3 flights in

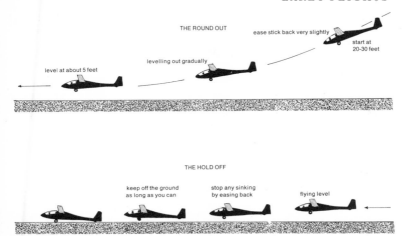

THE ROUND OUT

ease stick back very slightly

start at
20-30 feet

levelling out gradually

level at about 5 feet

THE HOLD OFF

keep off the ground
as long as you can

stop any sinking
by easing back

flying level

10. The round out, hold off and landing. At about 20–30 feet a very tiny, gradual backward movement is made on the stick to start the round out. The glider is then kept just above the ground with a gentle gradual backward movement until it sinks slightly and lands.

succession and then not flying again for a long period.

The process of landing is very comprehensively explained in *Beginning Gliding*. The key points are as follows:

Look well ahead during the final approach, 100–200 yards ahead and not just over the nose.

Start the levelling out with a *minute* backward movement on the stick at about 20–30 feet so that by the time the aircraft is flying level it is 2–5 feet above the ground—*not* too close. (Fig. 10.)

The aim is then to keep the aircraft off the ground for as long as possible without gaining height. This is achieved by a gradual backward movement on the stick. If the aircraft begins to balloon (gain height) stop the backward movement and wait for a moment; as it begins to sink again you must stop it sinking by easing back gently. Eventually the aircraft will settle and touch down. It is an instinctive reaction at first to move the stick forward as soon as you see the aircraft

35

ballooning up, but if you do so you will fly back heavily into the ground. It is only when you balloon up 15–20 feet that a small forward movement is needed and then you have time to ease back and stop the descent. If you are trying to get down on to the ground you will never make a good landing. However, if you find yourself up at 10 or 15 feet and flying level, do not make any further backward movement on the stick until the aircraft has started to sink and is nearer the ground. (Fig. 11.)

Landing is the knack of seeing and understanding what is happening and of responding appropriately on the stick. It takes some practice because the sensitivity of the controls is different each time and because, as the aircraft floats along

11. Corrections when ballooning or holding off too high. Unless the height is more than 10–15 feet, do not move forward on the stick. Hold the stick still and wait until the glider starts to sink again—then hold it off with a gradual backward movement until it lands. If the ballooning is very high a *small* movement forward should be made to start a fresh approach.

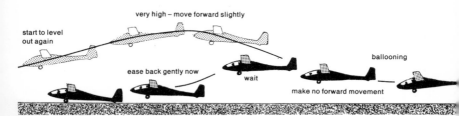

very high – move forward slightly

start to level out again

ease back gently now

wait

ballooning

make no forward movement

now ease back gently

wait

holding off too high

using up its excess speed, the controls become less and less responsive.

The airbrakes have nothing to do with the landing itself, but regulate the approach angle, and control where the glider will touch down. Regardless of the approach misjudgments, the glider must always be held off properly for as long as possible or the landing itself will be a bad one.

A premature landing means touching down at a higher speed in a more nose-down attitude and this leads to bouncing heavily unless the ground is exceptionally smooth.

During these early landings the instructor will be using the airbrakes for you, and if the glider balloons badly, he will reduce their setting to allow you another attempt at landing a little further up the field. Reducing the airbrake like this is a skilled business since if it is done just as the aircraft balloons up, it results in more lift and more height still. The correct moment to reduce the airbrake is just as the aircraft begins to sink again. This reduces the drag and gives a little more lift so that there is control for a further attempt at the hold off.

Once your landings are fairly consistent and the instructor no longer needs to make these corrections, it is time for you to take over the operation of the airbrakes. Trying to start using the airbrakes too soon usually causes even more difficulties. Ideally the whole landing should be done without any need to change the setting of the airbrakes.

After touchdown, a gradual backward movement will keep the tail down, reducing the loads on the front skid. Do not relax, keep the wings level and keep the glider straight with the rudder using the stick and rudder independently.

Points to remember

1. The correct attitude gives the correct speed and efficient gliding flight.
2. The attitude, controlled by the elevator, determines the speed; nose high—too slow and poor control, nose low—too fast.
3. Lean the stick the way you want to go.

4. Left foot forward applies left rudder and swings the nose to the left. Remember to relax your other foot.
5. Relax. If the glider is accurately trimmed it will fly itself.
6. Learn the order of the control movements for a turn.
7. Keep a good lookout for other aircraft but watch ahead as you apply the bank. Do not look at the wingtips.
8. Use the stick and rudder together to apply and take off bank.
9. Very little rudder is needed during any steady turn.
10. Do not forget the small backward movement on the stick during the turn.
11. Look about 100 yds ahead during the approach and landing.
12. Round out very gradually starting about 20 to 30 feet up, and aim to be flying level 2 to 5 feet above the ground, not too close. (These heights can be reduced as you gain experience.)
13. Keep just off the ground for as long as possible using a gradual backward movement on the stick.
14. Hold the stick still if the glider balloons up a few feet, then continue the hold off as it starts to sink again. Do not move forward unless the aircraft balloons to 20 or 30 feet.
15. After touchdown keep the wings level with ailerons and keep straight with the rudder alone.

Your notes on this chapter and on your own problems

Questions to ask your instructor

5

GETTING UP THERE

Launching methods, aerotow launching—positioning up and down, the low tow position, lateral control on tow, signals on tow, car and winch launches, cable breaks and launch failures

Launching methods

Of course, in a motor glider all the time you are climbing you can practise turns and improve your coordination. You may notice that while the aircraft is climbing the rudder is a little heavier to move and that errors such as forgetting the rudder do not cause quite such a noticeable swing of the nose as in a glider. The extra slipstream behind the propeller makes both fin and rudder more effective. When the power is cut off and the propeller is either windmilling or stopped, the motor glider handles much more like a normal glider, but still has rather heavier rudder loads. Changing the power also affects the fore and aft trim. Power off results in the aircraft becoming more nose heavy, full power gives a nose up pitching movement.

Always retrim the aircraft with the trimmer after any big change in power. It will be far easier to fly steadily if the aircraft is properly trimmed.

Aerotow launching requires quite a high standard of handling and if your training is by aerotow, your instructor may well do the launch himself until you are well over halfway through your training. This is often better than attempting aerotow too early, and becoming disheartened at your lack of progress.

In most countries aerotowing has superseded winch and

car launching, but if the cost of fuel continues to rise it seems possible that many more gliding clubs will revert to these very economical methods of launching. With winch or car launching, the launch is easier since the glider will more or less fly itself up the launch like a kite. The important things are to keep the wings level on take off, to get the glider balanced on the mainwheel with both front and rear skids off the ground, and to control the initial climb so that it starts gradually, and progressively steepens up into the full climb. Most modern gliders tend to come up into a steep climb by themselves and the pilot has to prevent this from happening too quickly by easing forward on the stick just after take off, but not enough to stop it climbing normally. If the gliding site is a small one and it is difficult to get high launches or to reach soaring conditions, the instructor may assist or even fly the whole launch to make sure of getting high enough to give you a chance to practise your turns. On a longer site or in good conditions you may find yourself doing the whole take off and launch on your third or fourth flight. When the initial climb is correctly done, there should be no particular hazard if the cable breaks at any stage of the launch. On your first few flights your instructor may take over or tell you what to do if this happens. Usually it just means a landing down the field and a long walk back.

Aerotow launching

Although the additional height provided by an aerotow launch gives more time for practising turns etc. and may make the circuit planning easier, the tow itself requires more skill than a car or winch launch. Until the student has considerable practice and can coordinate the stick and rudder movements smoothly, keeping exactly in position behind the towing aircraft is bound to seem difficult if not impossible.

Keeping position is a matter of spotting any slight change and correcting for it immediately; it is the knack of seeing the beginning of a movement and responding with a tiny correction on the controls.

12. Aerotowing.

1. On take off. Do not climb; fly level just above the towplane.
2. The normal tow position is just above the turbulent wake with the towplane a little below the horizon for a 150 h.p. Cub or similar powered machine.
3. A high powered towplane will have a steeper climb and must be positioned higher up above the horizon.

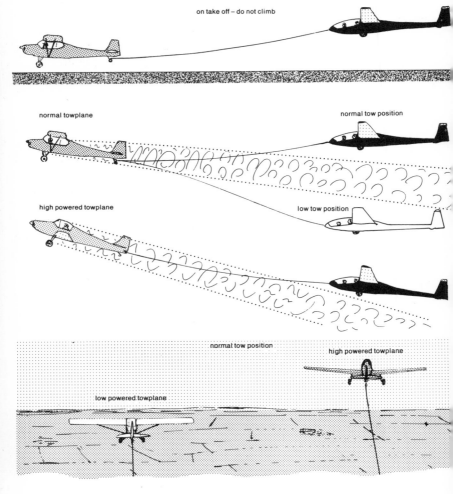

Because the launching speed is greater than the normal cruising speed of the glider all the controls are more sensitive than normal. However, the aileron is also considerably heavier. This often results in a tendency for the beginner to undercontrol the aileron while overcontrolling with the fore and aft movements on the stick.

Positioning up and down

The normal towing position is with the glider flying just above the turbulent wake of the tug. The exact position depends upon the type and power of the towing aircraft but if a line is taken through the fuselage the glider should be just above that line. The propeller slipstream and wash from the wings is always deflected a little downwards. (see Fig. 12.)

There are several ways to judge this position. Once the position is known it can be maintained by keeping the same view of the tug. For example, on the Super Cub, the position should be approximately with the top of the fin in line with the top of the cabin or with the tailplane cutting just above the junction of the undercarriage and wing struts.

On a clear day the glider may be positioned so that the tug appears in a constant position relative to the horizon. For low powered tow planes such as the Super Cub, Citabria etc., the position is with the tug just below the horizon. More powerful tugs will be above the horizon because of their much steeper climbing angle.

On some gliders it is a simple matter to choose a point at the top of the instrument panel or a suitable mark on the canopy well forward and keep it steady in relation to the tug. As soon as the tow plane appears to start to move up or down a small correction is required to stop it immediately. These tiny corrections need to be a small movement followed by a countermove to prevent too great a change. The secret is to detect the beginning of any movement of the towplane and to move the control in time to prevent the glider from getting seriously out of position.

Just after take off there is always a tendency to be left below the tow plane when it starts to climb after gaining speed. The glider must be kept clear of the slipstream or it becomes very difficult to control laterally. In the normal tow position the glider should always keep above the fore and aft axis of the tow plane.

The low tow position

There is an alternative position for the glider known as the low tow position, and this is popular in some countries. The towing aircraft is allowed to climb above the glider after take off so that the glider flies through the slipstream until it is just below the turbulent wake. In this position it is a little easier to keep the tow rope under a constant load so that there is no snatching, but it is usual to move up into the normal towing position before releasing the rope.

Lateral control on tow

If the wings were kept parallel with the wings of the tow plane, the glider would stay close to the correct position all the time. Usually the problems start when one wing drops and the pilot fails to bring it level again immediately. This pulls the glider off to one side. By this time the pilot's late correction begins to take effect and the glider banks and swings back towards the correct position. But again his correction is always too little and too late and the oscillation (swinging from side to side) continues. One simple solution to this problem is to concentrate on bringing the wings level instead of trying to get back to the correct position. This stops the oscillations immediately and allows the glider (and pilot) to settle down. If the wings are held level the pull of the rope gradually brings the glider back into line. When the tug begins to bank into a turn, the glider follows a few seconds later by using the same angle of bank and keeping in position.

When the glider pilot wants to release it is just a matter of releasing the tow rope while the glider is in the normal tow position. As soon as the tow rope is seen to have gone, the glider is pulled up into a climbing turn. This takes it well clear of the rope and the tug. In Great Britain the turn can be in either direction after release but in most other countries, including the USA, it is mandatory to turn off to the right.

It is quite normal to find the task of aerotowing accurately quite impossible on the first few tows. The knack comes quite suddenly to most beginners and it is just a matter of practice and experience—so do not despair! The secret is really in anticipating the movements of the glider in relation to the tow plane. Once you have acquired the knack of keeping station you may be given practice at moving from the high to the low tow positions and various other exercises to improve your skill.

Signals on tow

A careless cockpit check may result in the pilot failing to lock the airbrakes so that they open during take off. This may prevent a safe climb so that the glider has to be ordered to release or even jettisoned. If time allows, the tow pilot will signal by 'fanning' the rudder from side to side. On seeing this signal or at any time that the handling of the glider seems abnormal or the rate of climb lower than usual, check the airbrakes. If the tow pilot has a problem he will rock his wings violently from side to side (known as a wave off) and you must release at once. If you find that you cannot release the rope, pull out to the left and tell the tow pilot by rocking your wings and yawing. He will then release his end allowing you to return to the field.

Car and winch launches

Both car and winch tows provide a very simple way of launching a glider to about 1000 feet and this is high enough in a modern machine to have a good chance of finding a thermal before having to rejoin the circuit and land. This is ideal for training purposes, where the student needs circuit planning and landing practice rather than soaring.

There is nothing dangerous about these ways of launching a glider but accidents do occur with pilots who are unfamiliar with wire launches or who get out of practice. The winch or tow car driver also needs to know what to do and it is dangerous to attempt these kinds of launches without some previous experience, ideally dual with a competent instructor. The launching speed is controlled by the driver and not the pilot and the launch must be abandoned if it becomes too slow or if it exceeds the maximum winch launch speed. Excessive speeds and poor launches are usually caused by the pilot holding the glider down instead of making a smooth, progressive change into the full climbing angle.

During the take off run the wings must be kept level, while the glider is balanced on the mainwheel with the tail just off the ground. Any scraping of the nose skid will indicate the need to lift the nose a little and will delay the take off, whereas the noise of the tail touching indicates that the glider is being pulled off the ground prematurely at a marginally low airspeed. Except in a crosswind the glider will have little tendency to swing because the pull on the cable tends to keep it straight. If the glider is held with the tail just off the ground it will leave the ground as it reaches a safe flying speed, making it an easy matter for the pilot to control the initial climb.

Obviously the glider must not be allowed to climb steeply until it has reached a safe height and speed, and with car launching this takes a little longer than with a winch because of the lower acceleration of the car. (Fig. 13.) The pilot controls the angle of climb, only allowing it to steepen gradually once the speed is adequate (above normal cruising speed). In most modern machines the position of the cable release hook, below the fuselage and only just ahead of the centre of gravity, produces a tendency for the glider to go up far too steeply. The pilot usually has to control this at first with a forward pressure on the stick, relaxing it gradually to allow the angle of climb to change smoothly. About halfway up the launch the pull of the cable tends to restrict the climbing angle and the pilot has to pull back more and more

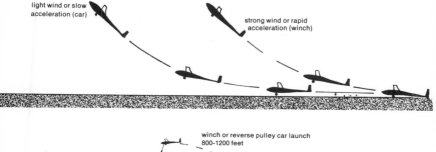

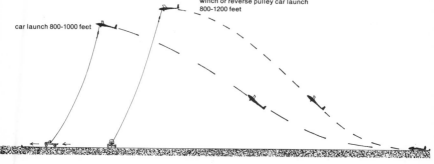

13. Launches. The rate at which the angle of climb can be increased after take off depends on the acceleration and wind strength. Winch launches give better acceleration and greater height than car launches.

to keep the glider climbing. Near the top of the launch it becomes difficult to maintain the climbing angle, and with the winch and reverse-pulley system of launching the nose is actually pulled down into level flight.

The top of the launch is signalled to the glider pilot by the car or winch driver cutting the power so that the pull of the cable ceases. At this moment the nose will tend to rise and the noise of the airflow decreases. It takes a few launches to learn to recognise these signs. The nose should be lowered immediately to just below the normal flying position and the release knob should be pulled *twice hard* to drop the cable. In some cases the cable may release itself automatically if the glider is high above the winch or car but it is still essential to

47

operate the release in case there has been a cable break and the glider is trailing a length of cable which could get caught in trees or overhead cables.

If the wind is across the line of launching, unless some correction is made, the glider will drift off sideways so that the cable may drop out of the field. On most gliders the best way to correct drift is to fly the whole launch with the into the wind wing slightly down and the rudder *central*. This will pull the glider over to that side by making it sideslip.

Cable breaks and launch failures

With any kind of launch the possibility of mechanical failure must always be borne in mind. At all times, the climbing angle must be such that there will be plenty of height and speed to recover into normal gliding flight and make a safe landing.

The immediate action is to lower the nose, to drop the cable and to decide quickly if there is room to land ahead or whether a turn must be made. Speed must always be regained *before* using any airbrakes and if the failure happens close to the ground and there is insufficient time to check the air speed indicator, the airbrakes must not be used in case the speed is too slow. (Fig. 14.)

However, if the trouble occurs at a greater height, once you have checked the air speed indicator to ensure that the approach speed has been reached, the airbrakes should be opened immediately to prevent any risk of flying out of the field. If there is plenty of room to glide down and land ahead, this is always the correct thing to do. It is not really the height alone which matters but also the amount of room remaining ahead for a landing.

There can never be hard and fast rules about the maximum height from which to glide ahead since so much depends on the wind strength and the shape and size of the gliding site. A rather slow launch on a calm day will leave far less room ahead at any stage of the launch. Furthermore, on a calm day the glider will glide and float much further up the field.

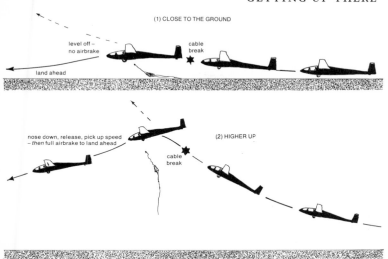

14. Launch failures near the ground. Level out, release the cable end and land ahead *without* airbrake. Higher up, nose down, release the cable end. If there is room to land ahead, pick up speed and then use the air brakes.

If, after lowering the nose and releasing the cable, there is any doubt about there being room to land ahead in the space available, or if there is obviously insufficient room, after flying speed has been regained the glider must be turned off to one side or the other. On a small gliding site the direction of this turn may be critical and the various factors involved, e.g. the wind direction and strength, and the shape of the field should always be considered *before* getting into a glider at the launch point. (Fig. 15.)

There is usually a definite advantage in making the initial turn to the downwind side of the field since it allows a longer approach into wind. Also if a continuous turn is made in this direction a full circle is not required and less height is needed.

If the landing areas ahead are wide it will be easiest to turn off, fly across wind and then to turn back into wind (known as an S-turn). On a narrow strip, however, the choice is between

49

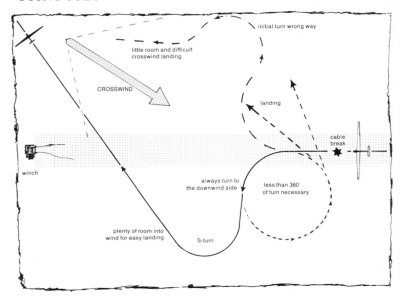

15. Cable break procedure in a crosswind. Turning off to the downwind side gives more room. Less than a complete circle is needed to land into wind. Use a well banked turn, checking the ASI frequently. A gentle turn uses up more height—perhaps too much!

going straight ahead or making a complete circle. This is because an S-turn on a narrow strip involves at least as much turning as a full circle, and results in extra problems if there are trees or obstructions along the sides of the strip. (Fig. 16.)

Once you have decided that there is insufficient room to land ahead it is important to turn off as soon as a safe speed has been regained. Any delay results in a rapidly worsening situation with less height and far less room available ahead for landing.

A snap decision as to whether to make an S-turn or a full circle is not required. After the initial turn it again becomes a case of looking up the field and considering 'Can I turn back into wind and land in the space now available, or must I keep turning?'

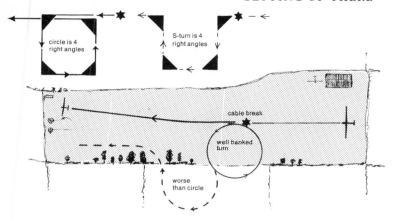

16. Cable break procedure on a narrow airstrip. Note that an S-turn is a bad choice as it involves as much turning as a 360° turn and obstructions on the boundary cause problems. The choice is straight ahead or a 360° turn.

It cannot be too strongly emphasised that a well banked turn must be used and that the bank, speed and height relative to trees and any other obstructions must be monitored throughout any turns. After turning off to one side it may become obvious that there is ample height to make an abbreviated circuit. In this case maintain the approach speed and keep rechecking the ASI so that there is no risk of running out of height and speed if strong sink or turbulence is encountered. In smooth air 150–200 feet will be lost in a well banked 360° turn.

The most critical situations usually occur in light winds after a slow launch, as this leaves the glider still climbing slowly further up the field without much height and without room for a landing ahead. In these cases, if the cable does break or the car or winch engine fails altogether, the choice of action becomes very limited, but there is sometimes the possibility of landing downwind if the field is large enough.

On most of the larger gliding sites cable breaks are simple enough to deal with and are an inconvenience rather than a real hazard. Cable break practice is a very essential part of pre-solo training, and where there are special problems due to the small site, early solo flying has to be limited to ideal conditions and a higher standard of airmanship is essential.

Remember that a launch failure or cable break can happen on any flight. Before *every* take off, plan your actions in the event of a cable break—taking into account the wind direction and strength, obstructions and the shape of the airfield.

Points to remember

On aerotow
1. Try not to overcontrol, use small firm movements on the controls.
2. Try to stop any change of position immediately.
3. Try to keep your wings level with those of the towplane.
4. Stop any swinging by holding your wings level and let the glider find its own way back into line.
5. See that the tow rope has released before turning off into a climbing turn.
6. Always check your position relative to the gliding site immediately after release.
7. Ask your instructor about the launching signals and emergency procedures and learn them.
8. In the event of an abnormally poor launch or wave off always check that your airbrakes are closed and locked.

Car and winch launches
1. Control the climb so that it changes gradually into the full climbing angle as a safe height and speed is reached.
2. Abandon the launch if the speed drops below the normal minimum cruising speed or above the placard speed for winch launching.
3. Correct for drift by banking slightly into wind throughout the launch.
4. Lower the nose before pulling the cable release twice hard to drop the cable.

5. Think before you fly. In the event of a cable break which is the best direction to turn off? Is an S-turn practical or is a full circle the only alternative to going straight ahead?
6. Never use the airbrakes until you have confirmed that you have regained a normal approach speed. If landing ahead and speed and height permits, use plenty of airbrake without delay.
7. Turn off promptly if you are uncertain whether there is room to land ahead, then decide what to do.
8. Use well banked turns and plenty of speed.

Your notes on this chapter and on your own problems

Questions to ask your instructor

6

STALLING AND SPINNING

Stalling, incipient spins, full spins, recovery from a full spin, low 'g' sensations

Stalling

The lift from the wings of an aeroplane depends on the airspeed and the angle at which the wing moves through the air (angle of attack). The faster the speed the more lift the wing creates and the greater the angle of attack the more lift is created. So to support the weight of the aircraft when it is flying at low speed it has to be at a large angle of attack, whereas at high speed the wing angle is very small.

The maximum angle of attack at which the air flows smoothly over the top of any wing is limited to about 16° or 18°. Beyond that angle the air becomes very turbulent and breaks away, causing very high drag and a loss of lift. (Fig. 17.)

In normal flight the wing is kept at relatively small angles to produce the necessary lift with low drag. At too low a speed or during manoeuvres, if the angle of attack exceeds the stalling angle the aircraft cannot continue in steady flight. The nose or wing drops and height is lost for a few seconds until the wing becomes unstalled. (Fig. 18.)

Stalling happens therefore because the angle of attack becomes too great. This can be caused by the pilot pulling back on the stick too much or too sharply and pulling the wing to too large an angle, or by the pilot allowing the aircraft to lose too much speed so that it sinks rapidly. This sinking results in a larger angle, thus causing the stall.

Unlike some modern jet airliners, when a glider stalls the

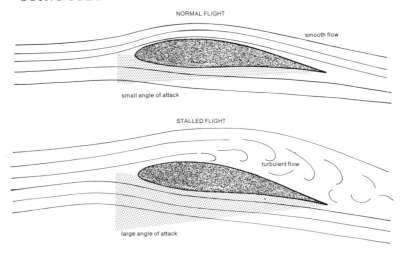

NORMAL FLIGHT

smooth flow

small angle of attack

STALLED FLIGHT

turbulent flow

large angle of attack

17. Normal and stalled airflow. As the air flows over the wing, pressure is reduced above it and is increased below creating the lift. At an angle of attack of about 15–18°, the airflow breaks up causing a loss of lift and high drag. This is the cause of stalling.

nose drops automatically and the wing tends to unstall itself by meeting the air at a reduced angle. The normal recovery in a glider is to relax the backward pressure or to ease forward on the stick gently to allow it to recover.

It is vital for the pilot to recognise the stall because any further backward movement on the stick to attempt to stop the nose dropping will delay the recovery and accentuate the loss of height.

In straight flight the symptoms of the stall are mainly those associated with flying very slowly—the low airspeed, quietness, poor response and lightness of the controls. The actual stalling speed in straight flight (about 30 knots in most training gliders) is raised during the turns and other manoeuvres. During steeper turns these symptoms may not be present because of the higher stalling speed and the stall is recognised mainly by the distinctive buffeting of the stick and the nose or wing dropping in spite of any attempt to stop it. If the nose drops regardless of a backward movement on the

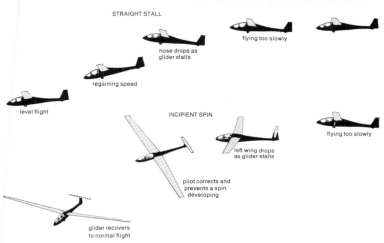

STRAIGHT STALL

flying too slowly

nose drops as
glider stalls

regaining speed

level flight

INCIPIENT SPIN

left wing drops
as glider stalls

flying too slowly

pilot corrects and
prevents a spin
developing

glider recovers
to normal flight

18. Stalls and incipient spins. At the stall the nose drops and the glider loses height for a few seconds until it regains normal flying speed. If one wing stalls before the other, that wing drops. This is called an incipient spin.

stick, this is a sure sign that the wing is stalled. When the backward pressure on the stick is relaxed for a few seconds, the wing unstalls and the glider can be levelled out into the normal gliding attitude almost immediately.

Incipient spins

If the glider is turning and the wing is stalled, the inner wing will usually drop causing a slightly greater loss of height. (Fig. 18.) At or near the stall the ailerons are very ineffective and therefore it is better to unstall the wing by moving the stick forward a little while applying opposite rudder (right rudder if the left wing drops) to prevent the aircraft swinging further. After a few seconds the ailerons *should* be used to control the bank again and the glider can be brought back to level flight or into the original turn.

This dropping of a wing at the stall is called an incipient

spin and knowledge and experience of recovering quickly from incipient spins is an important part of learning to glide.

If as the glider stalls and drops one wing the pilot fails to recognise the situation and tries to stop the nose dropping by holding the stick hard back, the glider may drop its nose still further and start to spin. This is a downward near vertical spiral in which the wings are still stalled.

There is a very important change which takes place as an aircraft begins to stall. In normal flight any banking movements are heavily damped so that an aircraft is fairly stable and does not tend to tip over very far. However, when the stall occurs this damping effect disappears and the aircraft becomes laterally unstable, tending to roll over. Since it also drops its nose in the stall, the rolling turns into a steep downward spiral known as a spin.

19. Lateral damping and auto-rotation. In normal flight the aircraft is resistant to rolling movements. In stalled flight if a wing drops it tends to continue dropping until the wing is unstalled. A stalled wing is laterally unstable and tends to auto-rotate.

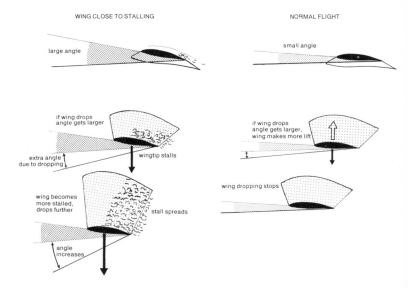

Figure 19 shows why this happens. In normal flight the wings are meeting the air at a small angle. If the aircraft is tipped so that the left wing drops, this movement results in a slight change in the direction of the airflow relative to the wing. The slight increase in angle results in a little extra lift which tends to damp out or stop the wing dropping further. The upward moving wing is also affected and makes less lift, helping to stop the banking movement. When the wing is stalled or nearly stalled however, a similar tipping movement may take the dropping wing beyond the stalling angle so that lift is lost instead of gained. This results in a further dropping of the wing, making the angle even greater. The aircraft then tends to roll over out of control.

If however the wing becomes unstalled, the spin stops immediately as the lateral damping comes back into force. At the incipient stage of the spin, therefore, a movement forward on the stick which unstalls the wing prevents any risk of a full spin developing. Failing to ease forward on the stick may result in a full spin or a second stall or incipient spin, losing even more height.

Full spins

Most gliders show a marked reluctance to enter a full spin if they are stalled in well banked turns whereas from a gently banked turn, particularly if too much rudder is applied, they will spin one or two turns losing several hundred feet in a few seconds. Some training and experience at entering and recovering from full spins is essential before going solo, although it is obviously more important to learn to recover from incipient spins and to prevent full spins developing.

Recovery from a full spin (Fig. 20.)

The standard recovery action for a full spin is as follows:
(1) Full opposite rudder and then with the aileron central,
(2) stick steadily forward until the spin stops,
(3) centralise the rudder and ease out of the dive.

59

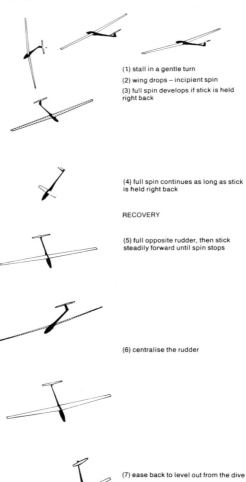

(1) stall in a gentle turn

(2) wing drops – incipient spin

(3) full spin develops if stick is held right back

(4) full spin continues as long as stick is held right back

RECOVERY

(5) full opposite rudder, then stick steadily forward until spin stops

(6) centralise the rudder

(7) ease back to level out from the dive

This should be learned by heart and applied as a drill.

On some occasions the application of the full opposite rudder may be sufficient to stop the spin but the stick must *never be kept back* or a spin in the opposite direction may occur as the wing restalls. If the spin does stop immediately, relax the backward position of the stick to about the normal flying position, centralise the rudder and ease back to level flight.

If the spin continues, move the stick progressively forward until the wings become unstalled stopping the spin and then centralise the rudder and recover to level flight.

There is no mystery about the causes of spinning. The aircraft has to stall, drop a wing and remain stalled. Any recovery from the stall at this point prevents a spin. In fact it is always the forward movement on the stick which is the vital action to recover from stalling and to prevent spinning.

With an unintentional stall near the ground however, the pilot will instinctively pull right back on the stick to attempt to stop the nose dropping—the worst possible reaction. If the stick is moved back and hits the back stop without any response, it is a sure sign of stalling and of the need to ease forward for a few seconds before bringing the aircraft back into level flight again.

Stalling and spinning is only really hazardous because of the rapid loss of height. It is caused by flying and manoeuvring at too low an airspeed, usually at a time when the pilot is distracted. It is therefore particularly important to monitor the airspeed indicator readings repeatedly every few seconds during the base leg, final turn and approach and indeed any time when the aircraft is within 500 feet or so of the ground.

It does not take much practice to become accustomed to detecting the approach of the stall with its distinctive

20. The fully developed spin and recovery action. The incipient spin can only develop if the stick is held right back. Recovery takes less than one turn of the spin and is simple.

buffeting and to learn to recover quickly and prevent any tendency to spin.

Low 'g' sensations

On some occasions as the stall and recovery is made the beginner will feel a low 'g' sensation similar to driving over a hump-backed bridge. This feeling is not an indication of stalling and must not be mistaken for it. It occurs whenever an aircraft pitches further in a nose downwards direction (including levelling out from a steep climb), or momentarily if it flies into strong sinking air or from strong rising air into more normal conditions. A large forward movement on the stick in normal flight or during a recovery from a stall will always make this feeling more pronounced.

Since most beginners associate this sensation with falling there is a tendency to assume that the aircraft is falling out of control when it occurs. This is not so. The recovery from a stall is almost instantaneous as the stick is moved forward and there is never any need to hold the aircraft in a steep dive. Any marked low 'g' feeling is an indication that the pilot has overdone the forward movement.

With further practice most beginners learn to overcome their natural dislike for the low 'g' sensation and until then, an unexpected stall or other pitching movement could result in a delayed or even an incorrect recovery response.

Points to remember

1. The elevator controls the angle of attack of the wing in flight and any excessive backward movement on the stick can pull the wing beyond the stalling angle.
2. Unless you recognise that the glider is stalled you will attempt to stop the nose dropping by pulling back on the stick. This will delay or prevent any recovery.
3. Easing forward on the stick allows the wing to unstall.
4. Stalling in a turn, the inner wing will usually drop.

5. If a wing drops, ease forward and apply opposite rudder. Then bring the wings level with the ailerons and return to normal flight.

6. To enter a spin the aircraft must be kept stalled after it drops one wing and starts to spiral downwards. Any relaxation of the backward movement of the stick will normally allow the wings to unstall. This stops the spin immediately.

7. Learn the full spin recovery action by heart, word for word.

8. Always maintain extra speed below 500 feet. Do not attempt to judge your airspeed but monitor the airspeed indicator every few seconds and correct any loss of speed immediately.

9. Keep alert at all times and remember that you cannot spin unless you stall.

Your notes on this chapter and on your own problems

Questions to ask your instructor

7

CONTROL OF THE APPROACH

Airbrakes, approach speeds, uses of airbrakes
(1) Using up height
(2) Controlling the approach angle, using an aiming point
(3) Speed control

Airbrakes

There are various types of airbrakes, but those in general use have two effects. They spoil the lift over a portion of the wing and they create extra drag.

Spoiling the lift is similar in effect to reducing the wing area. With less wing to support the same weight, the glider must fly a little faster. In other words the minimum flying speed or stalling speed is increased. In most gliders this increase is 2–3 knots, a small but—as you will see—most useful effect.

The drag increase depends on the type of airbrake. Spoilers, which are a simple hinged flap on the top surface of the wing are least effective. These are used on the older Schweizer 222, K4 two-seaters and some motor gliders. They require a progressive pull force to open them, are spring loaded and have no positive lock to indicate to the pilot that they are properly locked. They often cause a slight nose down trim change so that the nose tends to drop if they are opened quickly. This may be almost sufficient to prevent the glider losing speed.

Most other types of training gliders have the type of airbrakes shown in Fig. 21. These have a geometric overcentre lock to keep them closed in flight because the airloads tend to pull them open once they are unlocked.

Whereas spoilers require a pull to hold them open at high speed, most airbrakes require a firm grip and a positive push force on the lever to hold them in the desired setting and to prevent them opening themselves fully. Form the habit of keeping your left hand firmly on the airbrake lever all the time during the final stages of the circuit and approach. Otherwise you may find the airbrakes opening themselves fully so that you come down short of the airfield.

With both spoilers and airbrakes the nose position must be lowered as they are opened or the extra drag will cause a loss of airspeed.

Before learning how to use the airbrakes it is important to understand how they affect the approach speed needed for a satisfactory round out and landing.

Approach speeds

Although the rise in stalling speed is only 2–3 knots, a satisfactory approach with full airbrakes requires an extra 10 knots. This is because the drag of the airbrakes starts to slow the glider down very rapidly as it is levelled out for the landing. The following table shows how the approach speeds need to vary with the amount of airbrake.

Type of glider	Normal cruising speed, in knots	Minimum approach speeds for calm air, in knots		
		Full airbrake	Half airbrake	No airbrake
ASK 13	42–43	52 (allow 55)	48	below 40
Schweizer 233	35–38	45	42	below 35
Falke motor glider	45	52 (allow 55)	50	below 45
*				
*				
*				

* Complete for your own training machines

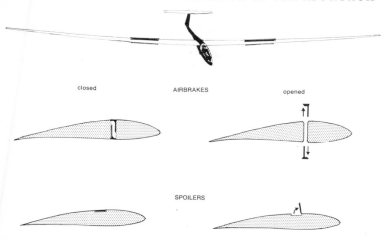

21. Airbrakes and spoilers. Airbrakes create large amounts of drag with some loss of lift and a definite nose down movement is needed to maintain speed. Spoilers have a similar but weaker effect and usually cause a slight nose down change of trim as they are opened.

If an approach is being made at 55 knots with full airbrake in either the Falke or K13 there will be adequate speed for a proper round out and float before touchdown. If the speed drops to 50 knots, the pilot must either regain 55, or if that is not possible, reduce the airbrake setting to about half. Otherwise he will not be able to avoid a heavy landing. If after a slow approach he balloons, it may be safer to reduce the airbrakes still further or to close them altogether to allow a safe landing to be made. Provided that the final approach was started with the airbrakes out and at a suitable speed, there will be a reserve of energy available to help if you balloon badly or lose a little speed unexpectedly near the ground. You can close or reduce the airbrake setting at any time since this gives more lift and less drag. However, if you have reduced the amount of airbrake because of ballooning or loss of speed *never* try to open them again until the glider is on the ground. If the airbrakes are opened the glider will rapidly drop 5–10 feet as it loses lift. If it is flying too slowly, opening the

67

airbrakes will cause a very heavy landing.

Do not be afraid to use full airbrake if you have plenty of speed, but use caution and limit the amount of airbrake if the speed is marginal. Always move the airbrakes smoothly and never jerk or snatch them.

Uses of the airbrakes

Airbrakes may be used in various ways and situations and it is very important to understand how and why they are used since they are essential for safe and accurate landings.

(1) Using up excess height. On some occasions it will be obvious that the glider is far too high and your one thought will be to get rid of some or all of the surplus height. Opening the airbrakes is a good way to do this because at any moment you choose you can close them again to check your rapid descent. If it is obvious that the final turn will be unnecessarily high, it is the normal procedure to get rid of excess height by using the airbrakes on the base leg. (The base leg is the last part of the circuit before turning onto the final straight approach for the landing.) However in windy weather, when it is very unwise to get much behind the downward boundary of the gliding site, the final turn into wind is made much higher than normal and the airbrakes are opened to throw away the excess height on the approach. Because of the strong wind the approach is very steep and little attempt is made at a precision landing because the landing run will be very short and errors will be small.

(2) Controlling the approach angle. In normal conditions, on the final approach the angle of descent is controlled by the airbrakes. Full airbrake steepens the approach and closing the airbrakes results in returning to the flatter glide. With practice the approach path can be very accurately adjusted with the airbrakes to give a landing within a few feet of a given spot. Small changes in attitude are of course needed to maintain the same approach speed when the airbrakes are varied.

Using an aiming point. The expert is able to make adjustments to the airbrakes to control both the approach and the length of the float before touch down. Adjustments during the hold off need special care because it is not safe to open the airbrakes further unless the speed is adequate. This can only be assessed by judging the response to small movements of the elevator since there is no time to check the airspeed indicator. Most beginners are unable to do this with any degree of certainty, so the inexperienced pilot is well advised to freeze the position of the airbrakes lever at 20–30 feet and to limit any changes to reducing the amount of airbrake to extend the float when necessary. In the same way it takes practice to be able to see the subtle changes which indicate whether the glider is approaching accurately.

22. Top: A glider seldom flies exactly in the direction of the fuselage axis.
Bottom: An object on the landing area ahead moves down relative to the nose if the glider is overshooting it or moves upwards if it is undershooting.

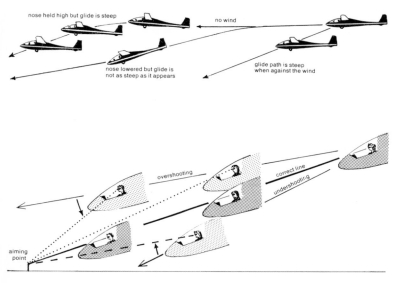

nose held high but glide is steep

no wind

nose lowered but glide is not as steep as it appears

glide path is steep when against the wind

overshooting

correct line

undershooting

aiming point

The final turn and approach is a busy time for the beginner and it is only some time after soloing that he learns to organise the thinking and flying so that there is enough time for refinements. There are very few gliding sites where an overshoot of even 200 or 300 yards is serious, and therefore perfect judgment and complete control are not necessary at this stage. It is important to realise that diving the glider on the approach does not prevent an overshoot. The height lost is turned into extra speed which must be used up during the hold off and this results in a very long float before landing so that an overshoot still occurs. When the airbrakes are used, height can be lost rapidly without gaining excess speed and the extra drag also reduces the float.

Figure 22 explains why it seems so difficult at first to gauge exactly where the glider will land. The flight path is seldom along the axis of the fuselage, especially in a strong wind. The more experienced pilot uses the 'aiming point' method, as illustrated, to detect whether he is under- or overshooting.

Just after the final turn onto the approach he selects the amount of airbrake he thinks will suit his position and height, and settles at his chosen approach speed. He chooses an aiming point some 50–100 yards short of the desired touch down point to allow for the round out and float before touch down. A convenient mark on the ground, a path or fence, is easiest to see. By noting the position of this object in relation to the top of the nose or some other obvious point on the canopy or fuselage ahead, any tendency to under- or overshoot can be seen.

If the aiming point is seen to be moving downward in relation to the nose, the glider is overshooting and will pass over the point. More airbrake is needed together with lowering the nose a little to maintain the approach speed. This, of course, necessitates noting the new position of the nose in relation to the aiming point before watching again for the trend. With practice an experienced pilot can guarantee to bring the glider down over the aiming point so that the landing is within a few yards of the chosen spot.

If the glider is tending to undershoot even slightly it is

disastrous to attempt to stretch the glide by raising the nose as this results in a loss of speed and falling short of the landing place. The immediate action is to *close* the airbrakes as this extends the glide without losing speed. When using the aiming point method on the approach it is a common error at first to watch the aiming point for too long, so that the glider almost flies into the ground. Do not forget to look out well ahead once the glider is getting down to 20–30 feet and is nearing the moment for rounding out.

Many approaches are too short to allow time for an inexperienced pilot to use this method but it does take the guesswork out of the business of making accurate approaches, and it is the only way to guarantee spot landings.

(3) Speed control. The airbrakes are seldom used as a speed control, but it is important to realise how they affect the speed. If the glider is approaching at an excessive speed (say 60–65 knots on a calm day), the extra speed will give a very long float above the ground before touchdown. This will result in overshooting and a long push back to the launching point after the landing. If the speed is excessive, full airbrake will help to slow the glider down and shorten the long float before touchdown. Normally it is necessary to lower the nose to overcome the extra drag of the airbrakes so that the approach speed is maintained. However, if the speed is already excessive the attitude may be held constant as the airbrakes are opened.

The pilot must learn to read the ASI very quickly during the approach, to check that the speed is adequate. If the speed gets a little slow and height permits, the nose must be lowered to regain speed. This cannot be done during the final 50 feet or so and the only alternative is to reduce the amount of airbrake. This helps to prevent a further loss of speed and allows a safe round out to be made at a lower speed than with full airbrake. (Fig. 23.) It should always be remembered that an extra 5 knots merely gives you a slightly longer float before touchdown, whereas 5 knots too little results in poor control with the probability of a heavy landing.

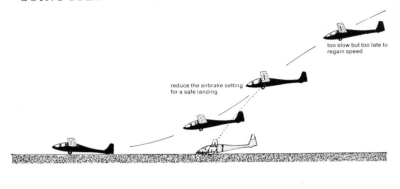

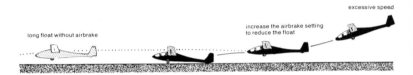

23. Using the airbrakes. If the glider loses speed on the final stage of the approach, close the airbrakes as necessary to avoid a heavy landing. Excessive speed results in a long float which can be reduced by opening more airbrake.

Similarly with rounding out a little too high or ballooning up during the landing, the loss of speed can result in a heavy landing. If the airbrakes are in use, the setting can be reduced *just as the glider starts to sink again* so that the reduced drag and improved lift will enable a normal landing to be made a little further down the field. However, if the airbrakes are closed partially or fully to avert the possibility of a heavy landing, on no account should they be reopened until the aircraft is firmly on the ground. Opening the airbrakes raises the stalling speed and always causes rapid loss of height for a few seconds, making it difficult to avoid a heavy landing.

On the approach the nose must be lowered to maintain speed as the airbrakes are opened. However if the airbrakes are closed or partially closed because of a tendency to undershoot the landing area do *not* try to lift the nose of the glider to avoid the resulting increase in speed as the airbrakes are closed. The increase in speed will seldom be serious and is of more benefit in helping the glider to penetrate against the wind to get to the landing area.

The ideal position for an approach in light winds is to finish the final turn at a safe height (about twice the height of tall trees as a minimum) and at an angle to the landing area which allows a spot landing using most but not all of the airbrakes. This gives a little adjustment either way and allows for the possibility of turbulence or sink causing an extra loss of height. An approach which requires little or no airbrake is potentially dangerous because there is no means of extending the glide path if any height is lost unexpectedly. In windy weather use the airbrakes cautiously because the approach angle is very steep, making the moment to start the round out very critical.

Points to remember

1. Consult your instructor and then complete the table on page 66 for the types of glider you will be learning on.
2. Use caution and limit the amount of airbrake if the approach speed is slow. Do not be afraid of using plenty of airbrake if you have plenty of speed.
3. Check the ASI readings on the approach and remember that 5 knots too fast is better than 5 knots too slow.
4. The airbrake setting can be reduced at any stage of the approach or landing. Use caution or avoid opening them close to the ground.
5. Lower the nose to maintain the airspeed as the airbrakes are opened but maintain the attitude when closing the airbrakes to prevent undershooting.
6. If the approach becomes slow, reduce the airbrake to prevent a heavy landing.
7. Never reopen the airbrakes if they have been closed or partially closed because of ballooning or a slow approach.
8. Try to arrange the approach so that the airbrake setting is constant for the complete round out and hold off.
9. Avoid landings with little or no airbrake.

Your notes on this chapter and on your own problems

Questions to ask your instructor

8

CIRCUIT PLANNING

Circuit planning, preparing to land, never low and slow, S-turns, landing out of wind, flying in high winds

Circuit planning (Fig. 24.)

The aim in circuit planning is to get the glider back to the final turn at a safe height and in a position from which the landing can be made at the chosen position in the landing area. This is made simpler by arriving at one side and opposite the landing area at a height of about 500 feet, so that there is time to assess the situation and to adjust the position and height of the final turn. If the glider is kept too close to the landing area there is little time for assessing or for repositioning before the final turn on to the approach. Whenever the height allows it is best to keep well to one side to allow for a proper *base leg*. Some instructors may refer to making a 'square' circuit since the glider circuit can be related to the 'square' circuit used by powered aircraft. This consists of flying straight and level at a constant height parallel with the landing run on the downwind leg, and of flying exactly at right angles to the landing run on the base leg before turning finally on to the actual approach. However, with the glider descending but meeting unexpected rising and sinking air, the downwind leg may have to be moved in or out to keep within safe reach of the landing area yet not too close to it.

Similarly, the base leg is not often made exactly square to the approach. Even a small patch of rising air encountered on the base leg will necessitate moving a little further back for the final turn, or an overshoot would become inevitable.

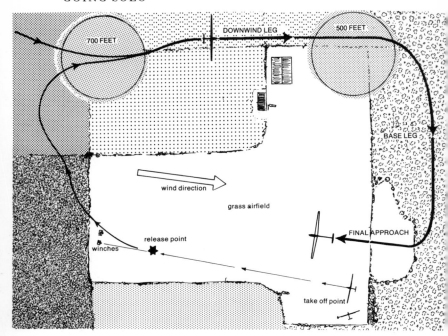

700 FEET

DOWNWIND LEG

500 FEET

BASE LEG

wind direction

grass airfield

FINAL APPROACH

release point

winches

take off point

24. Basic circuit planning. A glider leaving the upwind end of the airfield opposite the winches at about 700 feet will arrive opposite the landing area at about 500 feet ready to start the base leg.

A little experience soon shows approximately how much height is lost in normal conditions in flying down from one end of the gliding site to the other, i.e. on the downwind leg. It is usually 150–300 feet depending on the performance of the glider and on the wind strength. On most gliding sites in light winds an allowance of 200 feet, i.e. leaving the upwind end of the site at about 700 feet, will be ample. But in light winds on a long runway more height will be necessary for the glider to arrive back with about 500 feet opposite the landing area. Look across to your landing area and try to assess your angle to it as in Fig. 25. A steep angle indicates that you are either too close or too high and that you will probably overshoot your landing point. Any excessive loss of height which results

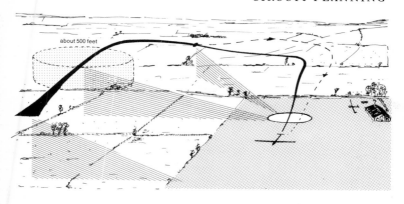

about 500 feet

25. Planning the circuit. Watch the angle to the landing area, particularly during the final stages of the circuit. Aim to arrive opposite the landing area at about 500 feet and always complete the final turn by a safe height.

in arriving back too low is a very real embarrassment since whatever happens the final turn must be completed by a safe height. This will necessitate cutting the circuit short, keeping closer to the field and making a 180° U-turn onto a final approach before the glider gets desperately low. The glider pilot must learn to recognise this type of situation and to abandon his original plans. (Fig. 26.)

Once the basic pattern of the circuit is properly established *the key things for successful circuit planning in a glider are to think ahead and to be decisive.* Flying downwind, for example, the glider pilot should not be checking the exact height so much as thinking ahead and considering whether he will arrive back opposite the landing area with too much or too little height. Immediate action, whether it is moving out a little or closing in, will usually mean that the final turn-in point can be reached for a normal approach. By the time the glider is opposite the landing area the pilot should begin to consider the position for the final turn. If there is excessive height some must be used up by adjusting the base leg to put the final turn further back and by using the airbrakes.

77

Again, during the final turn the pilot should reassess the position so that he is ready to use the airbrakes immediately if the approach needs to be steep. Here a delay of even 10 seconds will mean an extra 300 yards overshoot. At first, every beginner tends to get left behind with the speed and apparent complexity of needing to position the glider in the

26. Procedure when the glider is running short of height on the circuit. Close in to the landing area. At about 500 feet pick up speed and prepare for landing and turn in to land in the middle of the airfield if necessary. Do not leave the final turn too late, compare your height with trees or buildings and turn in to complete the turn by a safe height. Note that in the left hand circuit shown, the turn onto the base leg has been made early to conserve height.

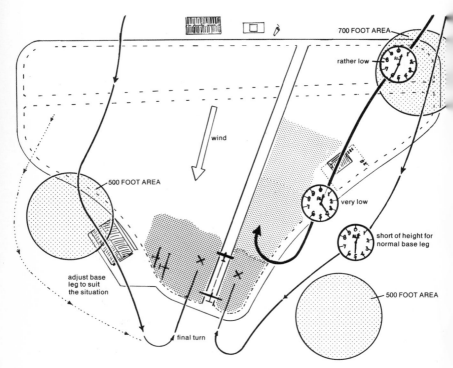

right place and at the right height for the approach, but with a little practice the idea of thinking ahead becomes established.

Preparing to land

The really important thing about the circuit planning is the decision to abandon all attempts at soaring and to prepare for landing. It is only too easy to go on searching for lift, or attempting to soar at low altitudes leaving insufficient time and height to position the glider properly for a landing. The beginner must take this decision at about 600 feet but local rules may dictate higher or a little lower than this for a particular site where special conditions prevail.

In order to reduce the effects of turbulence and of lift or sink on the glider, extra speed is essential during the last parts of the circuit.

With most training gliders this extra speed should be maintained for the whole base leg, final turn and final approach. With some modern types which require rather lower approach speeds, the extra speed will have to be lost again after the final turn to stop the glider floating a very long way after the round out. This is only necessary when the airbrakes of the particular type of glider are rather weak and ineffective.

Never low and slow

There is a very serious risk incurred by gliding slowly during the last few hundred feet. Any sudden loss of height caused by flying into unexpected sink or turbulence will result in being too low to gain the extra speed that is vital for a safe turn at low altitude. Within seconds the pilot may be faced with an impossible situation. If he attempts to convert his remaining height into speed there will be no height left for the turn. Alternatively, if an attempt is made to turn without the extra speed, the glider may easily become stalled and spin in the turbulent air near the ground. Once the glider is low and slow there is no solution and an accident is almost inevitable.

These disastrous situations can only occur if the pilot fails to make a clear-cut decision to get ready for the landing at a reasonable height. 300–500 feet is perhaps the lowest safe height to make this increase in speed. However, it is more usual to make this speed change at about 500 feet just before turning onto the base leg. In windy or very unstable conditions much more height is desirable and on airfields where power flying and gliding go on together, or where all launching is by aerotow, it is not unusual to gain the approach speed at the upwind end of the field at about 800 feet. In this case no circling or attempts to use lift are permitted below this height. You will be told about the local rules and how you should plan your circuit by your own instructor when you start to learn circuit planning.

The preparation for landing is often made in the form of a definite cockpit routine as an aid to memory.

However, most of the items included are a matter of general airmanship. If the wheel is retracted, this is lowered ready for landing and the flaps, if fitted, are set as required. (These items are not always found on training gliders.) The nose is lowered and the trim is adjusted to help maintain the approach speed. As far as possible the proposed landing spot should be chosen and the whole approach area should be checked and re-checked for other gliders and approaching aircraft. Most important, because of the probability of altimeter errors, the readings of the altimeter should be completely ignored for the base leg and final turn.

At this stage it is wise to unlock and open the airbrakes momentarily to check that they are not frozen up. If they are held closed but not re-locked the tendency for the airbrakes to snatch open is greatly reduced. From this point onwards the pilot should be constantly glancing at the landing area in order to assess the height and positioning. The airspeed must also be constantly monitored by quick glances since it is difficult if not impossible to judge speeds and altitudes accurately during this final stage of the approach.

The most common error is to forget to allow room for the final turn and for a reasonable length of straight approach.

27. Circling and the effects of drift. A well banked turn uses up less height and reduces the distance the glider drifts with the wind. Use well banked turns.

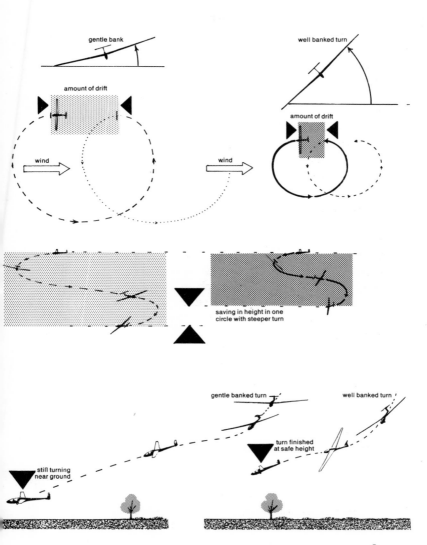

Most beginners keep the base leg far too close to the landing area so that, when the final turn is made, they find themselves right above the landing area and the actual landing is then a long way up the field. Of course in very strong winds this is not a bad error since the approach is bound to be very steep and the glider does not float far on the landing. In light winds, however, the final turn needs to be completed several hundred yards back and there is virtually no risk of undershooting.

Provided that the final turn is in approximately the right place at the right height it will be a simple matter to adjust the final approach for an accurate landing in the chosen area.

The planning and manoeuvring necessary to arrive opposite the landing area at about the right height can be resolved into a few simple rules. It is always far easier to arrive back with extra height than to try to be precise and perhaps to run short of height due to sinking air. Extra height is only an embarrassment if the glider is kept too close to the landing area. It is usually an easy matter to use up an extra two hundred feet by opening the airbrakes fully at the start of the base leg.

If it is intended to use up some height by circling, it is

28. The S-turn. Never turn or circle away from the field to use up height on or near the base leg.

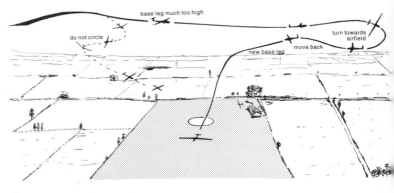

base leg much too high

do not circle

turn towards airfield

move back

new base leg

important to use a well-balanced turn to minimise the time taken to complete the circle. A gentle turn will use much more height and will also result in the glider drifting downwind much further. In sinking air a circle will usually result in a loss of about two hundred feet. It is wise, therefore, to consider whether this will be just an embarrassment or whether it will be dangerous. Once the glider is opposite or downwind of the landing area, circling to use up height is not safe and is bad airmanship. In one circle the glider may lose so much height and drift so far back that it may be out of safe gliding range of the landing area (Fig. 27). *Never* circle to use up height on or near the downwind boundary of the field. The height can easily be used up by widening the circuit and by using the airbrakes straight away. Moreover, the pilot has complete control over the situation if it is done this way.

S-turns

Although the use of S-turns is normally discouraged, an S-turn is preferable to making a circle downwind of the landing area to use up height and so turning your back on the landing area.

Figure 28 shows how to make an S-turn. If the glider is far too high to be brought into a reasonable position for a normal final turn and approach, it is flown on past the turn in point, dropping back behind the landing area slightly. A turn is made *towards* the airfield (*NEVER* away) so that the aircraft is in a position to start a new base leg from the other side. This time the airbrakes are used promptly, if required, to ensure that a normal final turn and approach can be made. It is most undesirable to make a further S-turn and it is always a sign of poor planning to do so. S-turns create a traffic problem on a busy airfield and should not be necessary. It is, however, important to understand that they are the only safe way of dealing with a situation like this which has been allowed to get out of hand. It is the safe alternative to making a 360° turn to use up height. However, during the rest of the circuit planning it is quite acceptable to circle towards or away from the field. On the base leg if your position is rather too close and too high, turn out and away, but do not circle.

In the case of winch or car launches the actual height achieved dictates whether the circuit consists of flying straight back for a landing, or whether there is time for a few turns in search of a thermal or for some practice stalls etc. The experienced pilot assesses the situation by looking at the angle to the landing area and so judging whether the gliding angle will enable him to reach it with plenty of height. The whole problem of circuit planning is made far easier by ensuring that a little extra height is kept in hand for the base leg. This enables a longer base leg to be made, leaving more time for assessing and adjusting the height with the airbrakes. Remember that, unless the wind is directly down the airfield, the glider will tend to drift closer or further from the field on the downwind leg unless it is headed off at an angle slightly to counteract this effect. The base leg will also have a head or tail wind component reducing or increasing the ground speed at this point.

Landing out of wind

If the landing area is wide enough, it is often possible to avoid landing out of wind by approaching diagonally into the available space. When this is not possible a crosswind landing has to be made. The object is to land the aircraft with no sideways drifting movement, since this creates large side loads which could easily damage the main wheel or skids. There are two ways of making a crosswind landing: the crabbing method and the wing down method. Most experienced pilots combine both systems by using the crabbing method and the same time keeping the into wind wing very slightly low (Fig. 29).

The crabbing method. The final turn is completed with the glider heading slightly into the wind and tracking down the required line towards the landing area.

The wings are held level and the glider is flown accurately with the rudder central. For the last 20–30 feet the wind

84

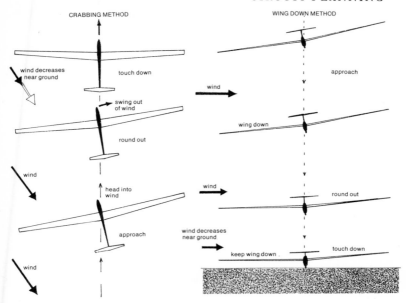

29. Landing out of wind.

Left: The crabbing method. The glider is pointed slightly into the wind with the wings level. Just after the round out the out of wind rudder is applied to swing the aircraft into line with the landing direction.

Right: The wing down method. The glider is banked slightly into the wind using the *opposite* rudder to prevent it turning. The approach is continued, gradually reducing the bank for the hold off and touch down.

strength begins to decrease because of the wind gradient, and the drift correction can usually be reduced a little. The round out and hold off are made normally, but *just* before the glider touches down, the rudder is applied firmly to swing the nose into line with the aircraft's path over the ground. This ensures that as it sinks on to the ground there is no drift. At the moment of applying rudder it is also necessary to apply some opposite aileron to prevent the into wind wing lifting as

85

the glider is yawed. Once on the ground the into wind wing should be kept down slightly to prevent the wind getting under the wing tip and lifting it. Otherwise the other wing tip will touch the ground before the glider has stopped running. There is a very definite tendency for all gliders to swing into the wind when they are on the ground.

The wing down method. After the final turn the approach is made with the into wind wing down a small amount. The tendency for the glider to turn is counteracted by applying opposite rudder and this results in a gentle sideslip towards the wind. The angle of bank, which is never more than 5° or 10°, is adjusted to make the glider track along the desired landing run, keeping the glider pointing straight with rudder. Again at about 20–30 feet, the drift correction needs to be reduced until, as the glider is being held off, only 1° or 2° of bank will be needed. In this method, there is no last moment action. The landing is made quite normally in the slightly banked position.

As before, after landing the into wind wing is held low and the out of wind rudder is required to prevent the glider from weathercocking round into the wind.

Notice with both methods the pilot ends up holding the into wind wing down and applying out of wind rudder. Above all the glider must not be allowed to bank even slightly out of wind or it will drift very rapidly indeed.

Pilots have their own personal preferences as to methods but it is important to realise that if the glider begins to drift towards an obstruction during the last stages of the approach, the drifting must be stopped by banking away from it, *not* by using the rudder. If the area is smooth and clear the failure to correct for drift will seldom cause damage provided that the landing is properly held off.

Flying in high winds

In general the stronger the wind the more turbulent the air near the ground and the more careful the glider pilot must be. The limiting factor in deciding whether flying is safe is almost always the degree of turbulence rather than the wind speed. Most gusts result in the glider tipping over sideways and in marginal conditions this kind of movement may be too rapid to be prevented by using the ailerons and rudder. This can be dangerous when the glider is near the ground, particularly if it is already banked over in a turn when it is rolled by a severe gust. It is also very important to maintain an adequate speed so that if 5–10 knots of airspeed is lost suddenly in a gust the glider remains well above the stalling speed.

Of course the glide path is bound to be very much steeper into a strong wind because the ground speed is very low. The only hope of penetrating far is to fly faster and then to use the excess speed to float against the lighter wind close to the ground.

The glider must never be allowed to get into a position downwind of the landing area from which there is the

30. Always start the turn onto the base leg earlier in windy conditions. Allow for drift and make the final turn with extra height.

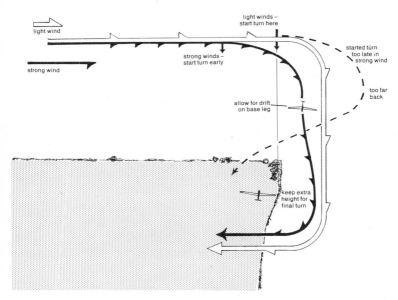

slightest risk of being unable to reach the landing area if sinking air or turbulence is met on the way. This means that the glider pilot must always keep a reserve of height in hand on the base leg and approach to allow for any sudden and unexpected loss of height.

When flying downwind the glide path is far flatter than normal because the ground speed is very high. On no account should the pilot slow down or the glider will be in danger of stalling in spite of the appearance of ample speed. It is the airspeed not the speed over the ground that counts.

A very real hazard is to fly to the normal position for turning onto the base leg before commencing the turn (Fig. 30). This can result in being far too far behind the boundary because of the drift during the turn. An error of only a few seconds in starting to turn can take the glider hundreds of yards further on so that if any sink is encountered in addition to the headwind, an undershoot will be inevitable. *Always* turn early on to the base leg in windy conditions. It is an easy matter to allow the glider to drift back on the base leg if necessary and this can easily be controlled.

Normally on the base leg you can prevent the glider drifting downwind by heading slightly towards the landing area.

The other real hazard in strong winds is the distance that the glider drifts as it circles. In a gently banked turn this can be many hundred yards in one circle. This means that in several turns the glider can be drifted back out of gliding reach of the landing area. It is therefore only safe to continue circling in very strong lift and even then any thermalling on or near the downwind boundary must be stopped in good time.

A very high rate of sink is often encountered in the turbulent air close to thermals. In most cases the loss of height is caused by sudden changes in wind speed giving a drop of airspeed for a few seconds. This is made worse if the glider happens to be flying rather slowly at the time since it will be almost stalled if it loses more speed. Flying faster minimises the effects of sink and loss of airspeed and ensures that the handling and controllability of the glider remains adequate.

There is always a tendency to lose flying speed and sink further when approaching to land in windy weather. The friction between the ground and the air above it reduces the wind strength so that at one moment the glider is flying against a very strong wind, whereas a few seconds later it is flying against a much lighter wind nearer the ground. This causes a drop in airspeed since there is insufficient time for the glider to regain the lost speed. (Fig. 31).

This *wind gradient* effect can be accentuated in the lee of trees and buildings and in the vicinity of hilly ground. The air remains turbulent for half a mile or more behind obstructions, sometimes reinforcing the wind gradient effect for a few seconds and at other times almost cancelling it out in a completely random manner.

More speed is essential to ensure that even with a loss of 5–10 knots there will still be sufficient speed for a satisfactory

31. The wind gradient. In strong winds there is a rapid decrease in wind strength near the ground. This causes a serious loss of flying speed during the final stages of an approach. Use extra speed in windy weather.

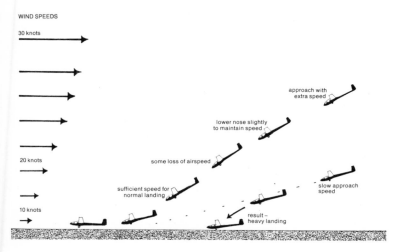

WIND SPEEDS

30 knots

approach with
extra speed

lower nose slightly
to maintain speed

20 knots

some loss of airspeed

sufficient speed for
normal landing

slow approach
speed

10 knots

result –
heavy landing

round out and landing. Even with adequate speed there will always be a rapid sinking as speed is lost during the last 100 feet or so. If the sinking seems severe, close or reduce the amount of airbrake being used to prevent a heavy landing.

In very gusty conditions it may be wise to let the glider land a little earlier than normal instead of holding it off for the slowest possible touchdown. If the airbrakes are opened fully just as the glider lands, this will prevent any gust from lifting it off the ground again.

A cable break during the first few hundred feet of the launch can be particularly critical since the wind gradient causes a loss of airspeed delaying any recovery from a slow launch. Always check the ASI and ensure that adequate approach speed has been reached *before* opening the airbrakes.

It is very unlikely that you will be allowed to fly solo in windy weather until you have 30–40 solo flights in gliders. Even a slight error of judgment can result in serious damage to the glider and instructors realise that early solo flying in bad conditions is not worth any risk.

Points to remember

1. Try to join the circuit well to the side and upwind of the landing areas with adequate height in hand. Check the wind direction and consider how it will affect the circuit planning.
2. Do not circle to use up excess height, unless you can afford to drift and lose 200 feet. Otherwise move out, using up the height by extending the base leg.
3. As you fly back downwind, check that the landing areas are clear and look out for other aircraft landing to assess where it will be safe to land.
4. If the circuit looks marginal for height do not let yourself get low and slow. Keep checking your speed and make sure that you pick up extra speed in time.
5. At 500 feet, or opposite the landing area (whichever happens first) prepare for landing: undercarriage down,

lower the nose, gain speed and retrim, unlock the airbrakes and disregard the altimeter. No more circling to use up height. Think ahead.

6. If it looks as though the final turn will be much higher than necessary, use the airbrakes and move back to reposition the final turn to give a longer approach.

7. Constantly check the airspeed, the angle to the landing area and your height in relation to trees or buildings wherever possible.

8. Lower the nose to maintain the correct speed as the airbrakes are opened. If the speed is adequate, do not be afraid to use full airbrake—if the speed is slow, be cautious and limit the amount of airbrake.

9. Correct for any drift on the final approach. Always bank away from any obstruction if you start to drift towards it.

10. Do not land close to other gliders or obstructions. Remember, the glider always swings or tends to swing into any crosswind. Allow plenty of room for drifting or swinging during the landing.

11. In windy weather always allow extra height in your circuit planning and especially for the base leg and final turn.

12. Always use a higher speed for both the base leg and final approach.

13. Always turn onto the base leg earlier in windy conditions. Never risk running short of height so that a low final turn becomes necessary.

14. Do not fly solo unless you have flown in worse conditions before and are quite sure that you understand all the risks.

Your notes on this chapter and on your own problems

Questions to ask your instructor

9

SOLO AT LAST!

Requirements for solo local soaring, thermal soaring, hill soaring, wave soaring, things to practise

Learning to glide is much more than a matter of learning how to handle the glider. To be safe a pilot must be confident about his ability, yet fully aware of his limitations. He must understand what he is doing and must have had sufficient practical experience at dealing with emergencies and awkward situations to be confident about his own ability to cope with them unaided. This requires an honest and mature outlook which we do not all possess when we start learning to glide. If a beginner is overconfident, the first solo flight should be delayed. Unless a pilot develops an honest judgment of his own ability and shows discretion in his flying at all times, sooner or later he will have an accident. On the other hand underconfident beginners have a different problem. It is not safe for them to solo until they have overcome their lack of confidence with extra flying experience and a real understanding of how and why things happen. In some cases this may take months or years and it is irrational for an instructor to try to raise the student's confidence by artificially boosting his morale with 'pep' talks. Unless the student is confident in his *own* ability any false confidence will quickly vanish if a difficult or unexpected situation arises. This can be the cause of panic and disaster. The beginner who already possesses a tidy, methodical and well-disciplined way of thinking has a distinct advantage since these qualities must otherwise be taught or assimilated during training.

At many clubs it is difficult to arrange to fly regularly with the same instructor and this can slow down your progress and hold up your first solo. An instructor needs to get to know you and your flying over a number of flights to judge if you are really ready for this step. If each dual flight adds further proof of your inability to fly consistently and safely without help, you are certainly not ready to solo. In this case if you persist in asking when you can go solo, the instructor will assume that you are grossly overconfident and in need of more training.

Before solo you must prove that you can plan your circuits and deal with any contingencies such as cable breaks, running short of height and stalling and spinning without advice or help from the instructor. Most clubs have a list of mandatory items like these which must have been done recently and which the instructor must sign off as completed. It must never be forgotten that getting off solo quickly is of far less importance than becoming a competent pilot able to fly safely in all conditions.

Statistically, first solo flights are safer than most other flights because the pilot has recently revised all the critical situations and is in good flying practice. You will not be sent solo until you are quite safe and the weather is suitable.

Local soaring

Your first solo flights are just the beginning of a new and exciting stage in gliding. Each day you will be given one or more check flights which, if satisfactory, may be followed by more solos.

You will be repeating all the important exercises such as stalls and spins, cable breaks and circuit procedures and with more solo flying you will gain confidence and improve the accuracy of your flying. It is particularly important to follow up your first solos with more dual flying and further solos *without delay*. This is the stage at which a gap of even a few weeks may result in a loss of confidence which will take much more time to overcome. Later on when you have a few more solos this is far less likely to be a problem.

Each gliding club has its own rules about check flights but

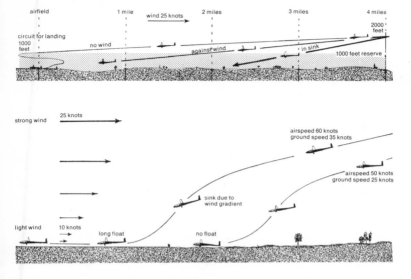

32. Local soaring. Keeping within easy reach of the gliding site.
Top: In no wind the gliding range is 4 miles per 1000 feet. Against a
25 knot wind the gliding range is halved. Sinking air together with the
headwind can reduce this to less than 1 mile per thousand feet. Allow
3 miles per 1000 feet and an extra 1000 feet for possible sink and for
rejoining the circuit.
Bottom: A faster approach speed *improves* the glide path against a
strong wind and gives a much longer float against the lighter wind
close to the ground.

it is quite normal for solo pilots who have passed the stage of a
daily dual flight before solo, to have a dual flight if it is more
than four weeks since they last flew. This might be extended
to six weeks if the pilots have more than twenty to thirty hours
of solo in gliders. On early solo flights it is essential that every
flight and approach landing is watched and if necessary
criticised by a competent instructor. This is the stage at which
good airmanship and judgment are being assimilated and
constructive criticism enables you to improve your flying.

It is also the stage at which unless you are careful you are
likely to become slightly overconfident. You may believe that

95

you understand everything but this attitude can only lead to trouble. Ask any really competent pilot or instructor and he will be the first to admit that there are vast gaps in every beginner's gliding and soaring knowledge, which only experience can fill. We never stop learning.

Local soaring means keeping within sight and *easy* gliding reach of the gliding field *at all times*. There should be no question of a possibility of landing away because of running into strong sinking air or being unable to penetrate against a strong wind. This is a matter of self discipline and of always playing safe by allowing plenty of safety margin.

As the glider drifts downwind gaining height in a thermal, it is a great temptation to keep circling too long so that it becomes doubtful whether you can glide back against the wind for a safe landing. You should aim to arrive back at the field with a thousand feet in hand to allow for rejoining the circuit. During training it is sensible to allow a maximum of three miles for each thousand feet of height available plus nothing for the last thousand feet. In other words you can be 6 miles away from the gliding site at 3000 feet or above (Fig. 32). Of course you will need more height if the final glide is against the wind and if this is the case you must fly faster than normal to help your progress over the ground.

If the visibility is poor, keep the airfield itself in sight at all times and keep clear of cloud and thick smoke. Shower clouds often have very strong lift below them. If necessary open the airbrakes and dive away well below cloud base or you may find yourself enveloped in the cloud and unable to lose height quickly enough to get back to clear air. In most countries it is illegal to fly close to cloud, besides being dangerous.

Remember that in the air you cannot park if heavy rain or snow makes it impossible to see ahead (a glider does not have windscreen wipers like a car).

Do not get cut off from your field by heavy showers—they are dangerous. Get down before a shower reaches the field, but be careful and check the windsock as the wind may be squally and in an unexpected direction.

One of the most serious hazards in gliding will always be

the risk of collision. Train yourself to look around constantly and take avoiding action immediately you see any potential danger. Good airmanship includes good manners and no other glider should ever have to take rapid avoiding action if you are alert and think about your relative movements in good time.

Choose your touchdown spot before each landing and really try to make every landing perfect and on the chosen spot. Be super-critical about the accuracy of your turns; no slip or skid, speed within 1–2 knots of the ideal and all the time keep that lookout.

When you cannot fly, read about gliding and soaring; you will always find many things to think about. Look through your log book and relive your failures and successes; watch the clouds and learn to recognise the subtle changes in the weather; help launch your friends and retrieve them when they land out. It will be your turn soon and you will need their help.

This is the way to become a real pundit.

Thermal soaring (Fig. 33)

Thermal soaring is the easiest and safest way of gaining height since thermals are at their best in relatively light winds.

No attempt should be made to use thermals below about 600 feet because a sudden loss of height caused by failing to contact the lift properly might leave the glider in a critical position. Many club rules specify a much greater height minimum than this.

Cumulus clouds are a sure indication of good thermal activity and the glider pilot learns to recognise which clouds are likely to be developing. These will probably have usable thermals under them. The height of these clouds varies enormously from day to day and with the climate. In Great Britain for example, the cloud base on a good soaring day will start at about 2000 feet in the early morning and will rise to about 5000 feet by mid afternoon. In many parts of the USA and in Australia and South Africa the cloud base may be at 10

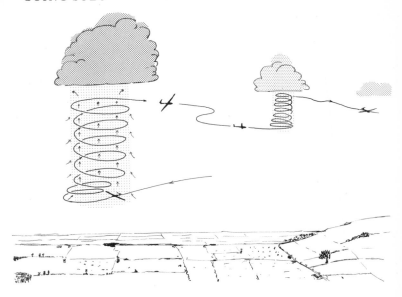

33. Soaring in thermals. Huge invisible bubbles of buoyant, warm air rise to provide the main source of lift for gliders. The glider circles tightly to keep in the strongest lift.

to 15000 feet, a soaring pilot's dream of heaven!

The variometer, a very sensitive rate of climb indicator, shows the pilot that the glider has flown into rising air and he then circles tightly to try to keep within the area of lift. Once the beginner is able to circle accurately at a steady speed it is not difficult to learn to find and centre in thermals. A well banked turn is usually better because it allows the complete circle to be in the stronger core of the thermal. Flying too fast results in a higher rate of sink and spoils the climb. It also increases the radius of turn so that it is difficult to keep inside the best area of lift. Any variation in either the angle of bank or speed upsets the circle so that the glider moves out of the limited area of the thermal. All the time the glider circles it is drifting with the wind and it is not safe to let it drift much downwind of the airfield or it may be impossible to penetrate back against the wind. Usually a thermal is surrounded by strong sinking air so that the height gained may be lost very quickly on the way back. The air in the thermal is often turbulent and this makes it a problem to fly accurately at low speed in a well banked turn.

A circling glider attracts other gliders looking for lift so that it is dangerous to attempt to circle without keeping a constant lookout.

Since any severe gust may leave the glider semi-stalled and on the verge of an incipient spin, it is essential for every pilot to be able to recognise stalling in turns and to make a prompt recovery without losing more than a few feet. When joining a thermal always turn in the *same* direction as any other glider nearby.

Hill soaring (Fig. 34)

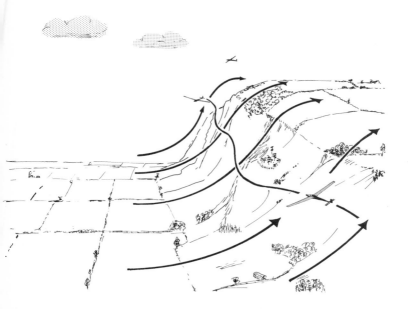

34. Hill soaring. Gliders are flown to and fro along the face of the hill using the effect of the wind blowing up and over the hill.

Many gliding sites are situated near ridges of hills so that when the wind is in a favourable direction, the gliders can soar in the rising air just ahead of the hill face. A site at the bottom of a ridge has the advantage that soaring can be attempted in much lighter winds with the gliders able to land easily if they cannot maintain height. These sites usually have problems if the wind is blowing the other way when no hill soaring is possible and the launching and landing areas are in the extreme turbulence in the lee of the hill.

When the site is at the top of the hill there is a constant risk of a landing in the valley if the wind drops. Soaring just above the top of the ridge is not safe since at least 400 feet is needed for a safe circuit and landing. In windy conditions when the ridge is working the landing area is usually in the turbulent curl over area behind the crest of the hill. Unless the hill lift is left with plenty of height and speed this area of turbulence and sink can result in such rapid loss of height that a safe landing is practically impossible. In fact the curl over often causes such a rapid loss of height that it is a rule at hill sites like this *never* to fly behind the downwind boundary on the base leg if a ridge wind is blowing. Solo flying is usually limited to the more experienced and skilled pilots.

The position of the best hill lift varies slightly from day to day. The glider must always be kept in a position from which, if height is lost very rapidly, the glider is not left falling into the hill top or onto the face of the ridge. Figure 34 shows the area and normally it is best to work out away from the hill side as height is gained.

The glider flies into wind just ahead of the crest of the hill. By turning slightly across wind it drifts along the ridge, gaining height until it is at about twice the height of the hill top. *All* turns are initiated by turning out away from the hillside towards the wind. This is vital because any turn the other way would result in the glider drifting back over the hill top into the curl over. From this position it is usually impossible to penetrate back against the wind to reach the lift and a crash landing on the hill top is almost inevitable.

You will be shown special procedures for the circuit

35. Lee waves. On some occasions the airflow over hills or mountains forms a wave system providing areas of rising air on each wave and going up to great heights.

planning when there is a ridge wind and these must be carefully observed. At the hilltop sites, it is essential to gain extra speed before leaving the hill lift and to have sufficient height to allow for the rapid height losses which may occur.

Wave soaring (Fig. 35)

In many ways techniques for wave soaring are similar to flying on a ridge. The position of the upcurrent is not clearly defined but can sometimes be deduced by the position of any cloud formed by the wave.

The wave lift itself is generally exceptionally smooth but in the lower regions there may be very severe turbulence in what is known as the rotor. This is no place for an inexperienced pilot! Very often at hill sites a wave system from other hills comes into phase with the hill lift. When this happens the gliders are able to climb to great heights by transferring from the hill lift to the main wave system.

With all the methods of soaring it is only too easy to over-concentrate on the soaring and to leave insufficient height to rejoin the circuit for a simple approach and landing. This can lead to difficulties, or even to being unable to get back into the gliding site.

During training the beginner must learn the need for caution at all times. There is no room in a gliding club for a careless or over-confident pilot who thinks he knows it all.

Things to practise and hints on becoming a better pilot

Fly on every day you can—calm or windy, dual or solo. There is no substitute for flying experience. Never refuse a flight.

When the weather is good and the soaring is easy, practise sideslipping, stalls, incipient spins and full spins to lose height. In good soaring conditions practise picking up thermals by descending to below 1500 feet before attempting to find new lift.

At a safe height practise steep turns, keeping the speed down to the minimum required for good handling with no buffeting. Try turning and slowing down until the pre-stall buffet begins, and then circle 3–4 knots above that speed.

Practise stalling in the turn and recovering to the same turn with a minimum loss of height and without losing the thermal.

Practise entering a well banked turn quickly and accurately and changing the angle of bank and reversing the turn without gaining or losing speed.

Train yourself to read the ASI, altimeter and variometer at a glance, retaining the image of all the readings in your mind and analysing them while you are looking round.

Every landing should be a test of accuracy in which you

choose your touchdown point and explain to yourself why the landing was beyond the point. It should be unforgivable to land short of the chosen point since the airbrake setting can always be reduced to extend the float however low the glider is flying.

Try to keep in good flying practice during the winter. In non-soarable conditions practise various types of approaches and landings. Perfect your cross wind landings, full-brake and no-brake landings and side slipping (once you have approval to do it).

Think before you fly. What shall I practise on this flight? How strong is the wind? What is the best area to search for lift or the best direction for the circuit? What approach speed shall I use? What shall I do if the cable breaks?

When the weather is too bad to fly listen to the instructors and expert pilots talking. Advice and help is free to those who lend a hand. Helping an expert to rig always earns its reward in terms of valuable hints and tips. However, beware the club bore who talks rubbish and seldom if ever flies—you will not learn much from him!

It helps to re-read your books because you always notice new points related to your flying which have become significant with the growth of your experience.

Every pilot should learn to act as the launch point controller or duty pilot, and should be able to help speed up the launching by setting an example and by helping the beginners to help where help is needed.

Remember that you cannot be a loner in gliding. You will need help from others. The best way to get help is to offer it.

The future

After solo comes a stage of gaining experience and becoming really proficient at soaring. It is not enough to be able to fly well and make spot landings on your gliding site. You must have enough experience to think clearly and to fly safely in difficult conditions and when, perhaps, you are faced with a landing into a small field over obstructions. Of course you would not choose such a field unless you had to, but under pressure your flying and judgment must not suffer.

Usually this takes a minimum of 30–40 hours of solo flying and most clubs do not send their pilots across country with much less than this, even if the pilot's flying is above the average. During this period of local soaring you should gain experience in recognising the type of crops in the fields below as they change throughout the seasons.

You should become familiar with the flying maps and with the principles of map reading and simple navigation. The Bronze 'C' tests in Great Britain and the Glider Pilot's Licence in other countries ensures that you read and learn the basic facts about Aviation Law and the rules of the air.

Above all you must learn your own limitations as a glider pilot.

You will never be bored with soaring because no two glider flights are ever alike and no matter how experienced you become there will always be more to learn.

FURTHER READING

Beginning Gliding, Derek Piggott. A. & C. Black Ltd, London. Contains very complete explanations and help for the beginner learning to fly gliders.

Understanding Gliding, Derek Piggott. A. & C. Black Ltd, London. How and why gliders fly, and facts that you need to know and understand in order to fly accurately and well.

Gliding, 4th edition, Derek Piggott. A. & C. Black Ltd, London. A handbook on soaring flight which includes comprehensive chapters on thermalling technique, hill and wave soaring, instruments, cloud flying, cross country flying etc., as well as training.

New Soaring Pilot, Ann and Lorne Welch and Frank Irving. John Murray, London. For the more technically minded solo pilot.

The Weather Guide, A. G. Forsdyke. Paul Hamlyn Ltd, London. An introduction to understanding the weather.

BGA Laws and Rules, The British Gliding Association. Mandatory reading for all pilots flying in Great Britain.

Sailplane and Gliding. A periodical published by the British Gliding Association.

Soaring. A periodical published by the Soaring Society of America.

Information on British gliding clubs is available from
    The British Gliding Association,
    Kimberley House,
    Vaughan Way,
    Leicester. Telephone Leicester 51051.

INDEX

Page numbers referring to figures are italicised